Editor
Janet Cain, M. Ed.

Managing Editor
Ina Massler Levin, M.A.

Editor-in-Chief
Sharon Coan, M.S. Ed.

Art Coordinator
Kevin Barnes

Art Director
Cjae Froshay

Imaging
Rosa C. See

Product Manager
Phil Garcia

Publisher
Mary D. Smith, M.S. Ed.

Take Five Minutes:
A History Fact A Day For Editing

Grades 3-5

Written by Deborah Hormann

Teacher Created Resources, Inc.
12621 Western Avenue
Garden Grove, CA 92841
www.teachercreated.com

ISBN: 978-0-7439-3051-2

©2002 Teacher Created Resources, Inc.
Reprinted, 2019
Made in U.S.A.

Table of Contents

Introduction

As students enter the classroom each morning, it is important that they are immediately engaged in an activity that is self-directed, self-explanatory, and motivating to them. Since it is often difficult for teachers to find activities that fulfill these requirements, this book was created to meet this challenge.

Each page of *Take Five Minutes: A History Fact a Day for Editing* contains sentences that need to be edited for grammar, spelling, capitalization, and punctuation errors. Below each date, there are sentences that describe an important event that occurred on that day sometime in history. The descriptions tell about a wide range of historic events that have changed our nation and the world, including the birth of famous authors, entertainers, and world leaders.

Many students will be intrigued by the topics they are editing and, consequently, they will be motivated to learn more about a particular person or event. For this reason, a list of appropriate Web sites and key words has been included for each month of the year. These will enable students to learn more about some of the important events that took place during that month. The key words will also help you select additional sites for your students.

Each day's sentences take approximately five minutes for students to correct. This gives the teacher time to take roll, collect homework, or set up materials for the next activity. An answer key is provided at the end of this book, enabling either the teacher or the students to check the corrected sentences.

By using the activities in this book, students will be motivated to come into the classroom each day in order to discover what happened on that day in history. Students will enjoy learning about important people and historic events, while using their language skills to "rewrite" history.

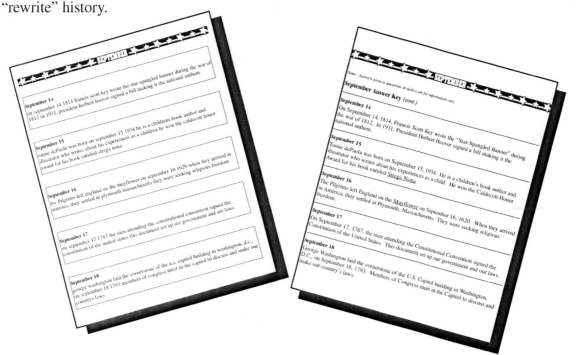

How to Use This Book

The sentences contained within *Take Five Minutes: A History Fact a Day for Editing* can be presented to students in a variety of ways.

- The sentences can be copied onto an overhead transparency and projected onto a screen when students enter the classroom. Students will then have the opportunity to begin work immediately by rewriting the sentences on notebook paper or in a spiral notebook, making sure to find and correct as many mistakes as possible. When completed, the students' work can be checked orally or in writing on the overhead. Students will enjoy the opportunity to use different colored markers to make the corrections on the overhead transparency. The transparencies can then be washed off and reused in following years. The same exercise can also be done using a chalkboard, dry-erase board, or large chart tablet.

- The pages in this book can be reproduced for each student in the class. Have students copy the sentences, making the appropriate corrections, on a piece of notebook paper or in a spiral notebook. As an alternative, you may wish to have students correct the sentences directly on the reproduced pages.

- Each page can be reproduced on cardstock. You may wish to reproduce the answer keys on the back of the activities to allow students to check their own answers. If you choose to make the tasks self-checking, be sure to match each activity page with the correct page from the answer key. Once the activities are reproduced, cut apart the dates to make separate cards. These cards can then be put into a file box and placed at a learning center for students to complete throughout the day. This is also excellent way to make the daily editing sentences available to students who have been absent or who need extra practice. Since this book includes activities for the 365 days of the year, you may wish to give the summer, weekend, and vacation dates for the year to students who need additional practice.

- If a poster-making machine is available, reproduce an activity page several times as a poster. Next divide the class into small groups. Provide a copy of the poster to each group. Then invite the groups to correct the day's sentences. The posters could be used occasionally as a variation throughout the year or as a way to model the editing process at the beginning of the year.

- Adjust the sentences to best meet the individual needs of your students. Some students may correct only one sentence each day, while others are able to correct the entire paragraph.

- Have students use the blank calendar grids (pages 80-85) to record their grades for each of the daily editing tasks.

Editing

Activities

There are several options for using the sentences in this book to enhance student learning and spark their interest.

- Use the sentences that correspond with the current date or as an introduction to a certain topic.

- Have students practice math skills by subtracting the year in which the event in the sentences happened from the current year to determine how long ago an event occurred.

- To further challenge students, delete part of the sentences and have them predict what information is missing.

In the following example, the name of the president has been omitted. Have students use the clues in the rest of the paragraph to determine that the information is about President Abraham Lincoln.

Example:

January 1

on january 1 1863 president _____ issued a document called the Emancipation Proclamation this document called for all slaves to be free many freed slaves choosed to fite for the Union army

---

- When it is a student's birthday, include a short birthday message about that person for the class to correct along with the editing sentences from this book for that day. Before doing this, make sure students do not mind sharing this information with the rest of the class. Another option would be to let the birthday person create his/her own editing sentence for the class to correct.

> **Example:** my name is jeremy brown i was born on febuary 25, 1993, in miami florida

- In addition to the editing tasks provided in this book, put individual or groups of students in charge of creating sentences to be edited for a given day. There is a list of Web sites (pages 67–79) and other resources (page 144) in this book that students may use as references for creating their own historical sentences for editing. You might also want students to be responsible for creating an accurate answer key and going over that day's lesson with the class.

Rules of Written Language

Using correct capitalization and punctuation can be difficult for many students. Grammar and spelling rules are not always consistent and things like irregular verbs and plurals can easily cause confusion. However, the ability to construct clear, concise sentences is an important life skill that students will need regardless of the career they choose. Today greater emphasis is being placed on effective written communication than ever before.

Editing *(cont.)*

Rules of Written Language *(cont.)*

The sentences in this book have been carefully constructed so that they are appropriate for third through sixth grade students. The types of errors in this book include the following:

Spelling

- The sentences in this book will often contain misspelled words. Sometimes commonly misspelled words will be featured.
  Example: *seperate* would be replaced by *separate*
- Sometimes a homophone will appear in place of the appropriate word.
  Example: *there* would be replaced by *their*

Grammar

- Some sentences will contain mistakes in subject-verb agreement.
  Example: *the boys was* would be replaced by *the boys were*
- Other sentences will have the incorrect form or tense of the verb.
  Example: *The document is prepared a hundred years ago.*
  Corrected sentence: *The document was prepared a hundred years ago.*

Capitalization

- Most words in the main section of this book are presented in lowercase. Students will not only need to capitalize the first letter of the first word of each sentence but also any proper nouns that occur throughout the paragraph. These include many acronyms.
  Example: *nasa* would be replaced by *NASA*

Punctuation

Periods:

- These will need to be added for both end punctuation and abbreviations.
  Example: *Dr Jones* would be replaced by *Dr. Jones*

Question Marks:

- These will occasionally be needed for sentences in this book.

Exclamation Points:

- Exclamation points are more subjective than most other forms of punctuation, and so when they appear in the answer keys for this book, they are more of a suggestion than a rule. Your students may use these marks more or less frequently than the answer keys suggest. Generally, it is better to use exclamation points sparingly.

Commas:

- These will be needed to separate items in a series, to punctuate dates within a sentence, and to separate introductory clauses from the main body of the sentence.
  Example: *red white and blue* would be replaced by *red, white, and blue*
- Commas will also be needed to separate two independent clauses joined by a conjunction, before a quotation, or to set off a parenthetical clause.
  Example: *Mercer Mayer the children's book author and illustrator was born on December 30.*
  Corrected sentence: *Mercer Mayer, the children's book author and illustrator, was born on December 30.*

Editing *(cont.)*

Rules of Written Language *(cont.)*

Punctuation *(cont.)*

Apostrophes:

- Apostrophes are often used to show ownership. Also, they may be needed when letters or numbers have been omitted.

  Example: *didnt* would be replaced by *didn't*

Quotation Marks:

- Some famous quotes have been added to these sentences; they will require quotation marks. Also, nicknames and titles of songs and poems need quotation marks.

  Example: *William Frederick Cody was better known as Buffalo Bill.*

  Corrected sentence: *William Frederick Cody was better known as "Buffalo Bill."*

- Periods and commas at the end of a quotation should be placed inside the closing set of quotation marks. All other punctuation marks, which includes question marks, exclamation points, semicolons, and colons, go outside the closing set of quotation marks, unless they are part of the direct quotation.

Italics/Underlining:

- Titles of books, movies, plays, anthologies, paintings, and sculptures need to be italicized along with the specific names of air-, land-, sea-, and spacecraft.

  Example: *Apollo 8*

  Note: Since it is impractical to write italics by hand, students should underline the title or specific names of air-, land-, sea-, and spacecraft in question.

Colons:

- These marks will only be needed occasionally in this book. They may be used to separate hours and minutes or to introduce a series of items.

  Example: the time *1130* would be replaced by *11:30*

Semi-Colons and Em-Dashes (Long Dashes):

- The use of these marks is never mandatory in the sentences presented in this book. However, if students are able to understand how to correctly substitute these marks for commas or periods, allow them to do so.

Parentheses:

- Parentheses are occasionally needed when punctuating the sentences. When information is extremely peripheral (or parenthetical), the use of parentheses is preferred over the use of commas.

Hyphens:

- In this book, hyphens are sometimes needed to conjoin compound words

  Example: *part time job* would be changed to *part-time job*

Slashes:

- Slashes or hyphens should be used to separate numbers in a date.

  Example: the date *9 8 98* would be replaced by *9/8/98*

  Also slashes can, at times, be used in place of a conjunction.

  Example: football and baseball player would be changed to football/baseball player

Proofreading Marks

Editor's Mark	Meaning	Example
☰	capitalize	they fished in lake tahoe
/	make it lower case	Five Students missed the Bus.
sp.	spelling mistake	sp. The day was clowdy and cold.
⊙	add a period	Tomorrow is a holiday⊙
ℰ	delete (remove)	One person knew the the answer.
∧	add a word	pups Six were in the litter.
∧̭	add a comma	He planted peas corn, and squash.
∾	reverse words or letters	An otter swam in the bed kelp.
V̓	add an apostrophe	The child's bike was red.
⌄" ⌄"	add quotation marks	Why can't I go? she cried.
#	make a space	# He ate two redapples.
⌣	close the space	Her favorite game is soft ball.
⁋	begin a new paragraph	⁋ to know. Next on the list

January 1

on january 1, 1863 president abraham lincoln issued a document called the Emancipation Proclamation this document called for all slaves to be free many freed slaves choosed to fite for the Union army.

January 2

on january 2 1893 the us post office issued the first commemorative postage stamp it was maked in honor of the four-hundredth anniversary off the discovery of america do you know any one that collects stamps

January 3

alaska became the 49th state on january 3 1959 alaska is knowed for its rich natural resources like oil gold and trees alaska is our most big state and it also has a longer coastline then any other state.

January 4

louis braille was born on january 4 1809 when he was three, he became blind because of an accident in his fathers shop he later invented the printing and writing system for the blind A sign on the door of his house reads he opened the doors of knowledge to all those who cannot see

January 5

george washington carver died on january 5 1943 he was born in missouri as a slave but he later becomed a famous scientist he experimented with peanuts and found over 300 different ways to use them, including soap plastic and paint

January 6

carl sandburg was born on january 6 1878 he was a famous poet and he writed many poems for children Sandburg said if poems could be explained, then poets would have to leave out roses sunsets and faces from there poems

January 7

the first presidential election in america took place on january 7 1789 the person who one that election was a general in the army and helped the united states gain its independence from great britain do you know who was elected

January 8

on january 8 1815 the battle of new orleans was fighted in the war of 1812 the battle was fighted to weeks after the war was over why do you think the soldiers didnt now the war was over

January 9

richard nixon was born on january 9 1913 he was known for being very good at working with foreign leaders but he is probably best remembered for beeing the only president who has ever resigned from office

January 10

on january 10 1946 people called "delegates" met for the first session of the united nations general assembly they met after world war II ended to try to prevent such a terrible war from happening again

January 11

on january 11 1964 the us surgeon generals report declared cigarette smoking dangerous for you're health smoking is dangerous because it can cause cancer emphysema and other lung problems

January 12

fairy tales have been around for hundreds of years but charles perrault was the first to right down the tales of sleeping beauty little red rideing hood cinderella and puss in boots charles perrault was born on january 12 1628

January 13

michael bond author of the paddington bear books was born on january 13 1926 he came up with the idea for paddington when he seen a lonely teddy bear in a store on christmas eve and buyed it for his wife they named the bear "paddington" because they lived near paddington station

January 14

the revolutionary war ended on january 14 1784 this was the war in which america fighted to gain it's independence from great britain after this war America became knowed as the united states

January 15

martin luther king, jr, was born on january 15 1929 he encouraged people to use non-violence to gain equal rights for african americans in his famousest, speech he sayed i have a dream

January 16

the us national aeronautics and space administration (nasa) accepted its first women candidates for astronauts on january 16 1978 sally ride became the first women in space in june 1983 abord the challenger space shuttle

January 17

benjamin franklin was born on january 17 1706 he was one of the first people to experiment with electricity he invented the lightning rod the franklin stove and bifocal glasses he also helped write the declaration of independence

muhammad ali was born on january 17 1942 he was a professional boxer who became the heavyweight champion of the world ali always said im the greatest he changed his name from cassius clay to muhammad ali when he became a muslim

January 18

on january 18 1778 explorer james cook discovered and named the sandwich islands they were later named the hawaiian islands hawaii became our 50th state in 1959

January 19

robert e lee was born on january 19 1807 he commanded the confederate army of the south during the civil war in this war, several southern states left the united states because they wanted to own slaves lee did not believe in slavery but he was loyal to the south

January 20

every four years a president is inaugurated on january 20 on january 20 1961 john f kennedy made his inaugural speech he said and so my fellow americans, ask not what your country can do for you; ask what you can do for your country

January 21

the pittsburgh steelers became the first foot ball team to won three super bowls on january 21 1979 do you now what other teams have also won three or more super bowls

January 22

on january 22 1905 the Russian Revolution began when russian troops fired on marchers at the winter palace in st. petersburg the marchers were protesting unfair treatment by Czar nicholas II a czar is similar to a king

January 23

john hancock was born on january 23 1737 he was the first person to sign the declaration of independence he signed it in large bold letters and said there! king george can read that without his spectacles

January 24

john sutter finded gold near his mill in sacramento california on january 24 1848 his discovery caused thousands of people to come to the area near san francisco this event is now knowed as the gold rush of 1848

January 25

on january 25 1924 the first Winter Olympics opened in chamonix france four a long time the Winter and Summer Olympics were held in the same year it was not until 1994 that the Winter and Summer Olympics were held in different years some of the sports in the Winter Olympics are skiing ice skateing and hockey

January 26

australia was first settled by colonists on january 26 1788 australia is the only country in the world that is also a continent it is best knowed for its coral reef kangaroos and eucalyptus trees

January 27

wolfgang amadeus mozart was born on january 27 1756 when mozart was six, he could play the violin and organ and compose his own music during his lifetime, mozart writed more than 600 peaces of music but he died a very poor man when he were 35

January 28

on january 28 1986 one of the baddest accidents in space history occurred the challenger 2 space shuttle exploded just after liftoff and all seven astronauts inside died christa mcAuliffe the first teacher to go into space was on board this flight

January 29

william mckinley was born on january 29 1843 he was the twenty-fifth president of the united states before he became president, he was a lawyer a congressman and the governor of ohio he was assassinated in buffalo new york on september 6 1901

January 30

franklin d roosevelt was born on january 30 1882 he was elected president four times he served in a wheelchair because he had polio as a child Roosevelt helped the country get back on it's feet after the great depression and was president during world war II

January 31

franz peter schubert was born on january 31 1797 he was a great musical composer and he writed over 600 songs during his short life sometimes he writed as many as eight songs in won day he died when he was 31

February 1

langston hughes was born on february 1 1902 he was a very famous african-american poet his most famous poem is called dreams and he often wrote about the african-american experience

February 2

february 2 is groundhog day every year in punxsutawney pennsylvania, a groundhog named phil comes out of his hole if he sees his shadow, there will be six more weeks of winter

February 3

elizabeth blackwell was born on february 3 1821 she was the first american woman doctor she earned her medical degree in geneva new york in 1849 she later started the womens medical college to encourage other woman to become doctors

February 4

on february 4 1902 charles lindbergh was born in detroit michigan he is famousest for making the first nonstop solo flight across the atlantic ocean he flied from new york to paris france

February 5

alan shepard became the fifth person to walk on the moon on february 5 1971 shepard and edgar mitchell stayed on the moon for 34 hours and even hit several golf ball off the moon with shepards golf club

February 6

babe ruth was born on february 6 1895 he became famous around the world when he played baseball for the new york yankees he held the record for 714 home runs until hank aaron hit 715 in 1974

February 7

laura ingalls wilder was born on february 7 1867 she writed the popular little house books she didnt begin writing the books until she was 65 years old the books are based on her own life as she growed up on the american frontier

February 8

jules verne was born on february 8 1823 he writed fantasy and science fiction books some of his books include around the world in eighty days 20,000 leagues under the sea and journey to the center of the Earth

February 9

william henry harrison was our ninth president he was born on february 9 1773 and died only 32 days after becomeing the president that is the shorter amount of time that anyone has ever been president of the united states

February 10

mark spitz was born on february 10 1950 he began swiming in the pacific ocean off honolulu hawaii when he was too years old spitz set a world record at the 1972 olympic games in munich germany when he won seven gold medals

February 11

thomas alva edison was born on february 11 1847 he invented the light bulb record player and copying machine he only had three months of formal education but invented 1100 things he always said the brain that isnt used, rusts

February 12

abraham lincoln was born on february 12 1809 he is most famous for issuing the emancipation proclamation, which freed the slaves he gave a very famous speech called the gettysburg address it begins four score and seven years ago….

February 13

on february 13 1635 the oldest public school in the united states was founded it was named the boston public latin school in what state is the city of boston

February 14

february 14 is valentines day this holiday is celebrated in honor of a man named valentine who was a priest in rome italy, when christianity was a new religion he was put to death for teaching christianity but was later chosen to be a saint

February 15

on february 15 1564 galileo galilei was born he believed that the Earth revolved around the sun even though most people didnt agree today we know he were write he also discovered four of jupiters moons using a telescope he designed himself

February 16

on february 16 1923 king tuts tomb was opened by archaeologists the tomb had been sealed for more than 3000 years scientists have studied a lot about the way egyptians mummified dead people to preserve the bodys

February 17

marian anderson was born on february 17 1902 she was a very famous singer and she was the first black woman to perform with the metropolitan opera company in new york she said I have a great belief in the future of my people and my country

February 18

clyde tombaugh, an astronomer, discovered pluto on february 18 1930 pluto is the outermost planet of the nine planets in our solar system it take 248 years for pluto to go around the sun and it can only be saw with powerful telescopes

February 19

on february 19 1878 inventor thomas edison patented the phonograph these machines played music by turning a crank and the sound comed out of a large megaphone edison is famousest four inventing the light bulb

February 20

frederick douglass died on february 20 1895 he was born a slave but he escaped and later buyed his own freedom he became an important journalist, statesman, and abolitionist he worked with president lincoln to end slavery

February 21

the washington monument was dedicated on february 21 1885 it was built in honor of george washington it is 555 foots high and is the tallest building in washington d.c.

February 22

george washington was born on february 22 1732 he was the first president of the united states and was the commander of the american army during the revolutionary war against britain he is knowed as the father of are country

February 23

on february 23 1836 the attack on the alamo began in san antonio texas this battle was fighted while texas were trying to gain it's independence from mexico The texans losed but later gained there independence

February 24

wilhelm grimm was born on february 24 1786 he writed german folktales and fairy tales he wrote hansel and gretel the ugly duckling and snow white

February 25

pierre auguste renoir was born on february 25 1841 he was an impressionist painter who lived in france he beginned his career painting china in a factory but later became a very famous painter

February 26

william frederick cody, better knowed as "buffalo bill," was born on february 26 1864 he was born in iowa and became a pony express rider and army scout he later organized a wild west show and toured the united states and europe

February 27

henry wadsworth longfellow was born on february 27 1807 he was a poet his most famous poem is paul reveres ride the first line of the poem is listen my children, and you shall here of the midnight ride of paul revere

February 28

the first shipload of gold-seekers arrived in san francisco california, on february 28 1849 gold is formed deep within the Earths crust it starts in liquid form because of the hi temperatures and then becomes solid as it rises to the surface

February 29

february 29 is leap year day the roman emperor, julius caesar, introduced a calendar for which his astronomers calculated the year to be 365 days and 6 hours long in order to make up for the extra 6 hours, they added a day every fourth year

(**Note:** There was still an error, so now leap years occur every fourth year except in century years not divisible by 400. For example, 1700 and 1900 were not leap years, but 2000 was.)

March 1

on march 1 1867 nebraska became the thirty-seventh state the state flower is the goldenrod the state tree is the cottonwood and the state bird is the western meadowlark

March 2

theodore seuss geisel, better known as dr seuss, were born on march 2 1904 his first book, and to think I saw it on mulberry street, was rejected by 28 publishers before it was finally accepted what is youre favorite dr seuss book

March 3

alexander graham bell was born on march 3 1847 he worked with people who were hearing-and speech-impaired during his research, he discovered a way to send sound threw vibrations this leaded him to invent the telephone

March 4

knute rockne was born on march 4 1888 he was the football coach at the university of notre dame and was one of the most successful coaches in football history he was known for his motivating speechs and always said win one for the gipper

March 5

the boston massacre occurred on march 5 1770 a crowd of american colonists were throwing snow balls at british soldiers and the soldiers fired, killing five colonists a monument now marks this spot

March 6

michelangelo was borned on march 6 1475 in italy he was a sculptor a painter an architect and a poet his most famous sculptures are the Pieta and David his most famous painting is on the ceiling of the sistine chapel

March 7

charles b darrow invented the game of monopoly on march 7 1933 when he first showed it to parker brothers, they were not interested however one year later they decided to market it the longest monopoly game in history lasted 70 straight days

March 8

march 8 is international women's day this holiday was first celebrated in 1909 and it is a national holiday in many countrys it is a day to honor women and remember there important contributions to the world

March 9

amerigo vespucci was born on march 9 1454 he was an italian mapmaker who sailed west looking for a route to asia but he discovered central and south america instead the continents of north and south america are named after him

March 10

on march 10 1913 harriet tubman died in auburn new york she was a slave who faced many dangers to lead slaves to freedom tubman said on my underground railroad, I never run my train off the track, and I never lost a passenger

March 11

on march 11 1888 the great blizzard struck the northeastern united states this storm left 50 inchs of snow in some states about how many feet is 50 inchs of snow

March 12

on march 12 1912 juliette gordon low founded the american girl scouts she formed the first troop in savannah georgia, and then traveled around the united states setting up different troops in all the states

March 13

astronomer william herschel discovered uranus on march 13 1781 it is the seventh planet from the sun and it has at least 11 thin rings around it the rings are much fainter then those around saturn

March 14

albert einstein was born on march 14 1879 in ulm germany he was jewish and came to the united states in 1933 to escape the nazis his research led to the development of television and the atom bomb

March 15

march 15 is known as the ides of march julius caesar was assassinated at a meeting of the roman senate on march 15 44 bc he was the leader of the roman empire over 2000 years ago

March 16

on march 16 1926 dr robert h goddard launched the first liquid propellant rocket outside auburn massachusetts it traveled 56 meters and the flight lasted 2.5 seconds his ideas helped to make airplanes and rockets possible

March 17

march 17 is saint patricks day saint patrick was born in england and was later captured and taken to ireland as a slave he escaped and became a missionary he tried to convert the irish to chritianity saint patricks day marks the day of his death in AD 461

March 18

president grover cleveland was born on march 18 1837 he was the only president to lose a reelection and run again four years later and win he got married while he was in office he developed cancer of the mouth and had to wear a handmade jaw

March 19

on march 19 1975 pennsylvania became the first state to allow girls to compete with boys in high school sports why do you think the state allowed girls to compete against boys

March 20

march 20 1854 is recognized as the first meeting of the republican party this party was founded to oppose the spread of slavery into western territories the first republican candidate to become president was abraham lincoln in 1860

March 21

benito juarez was born on march 21 1806 he is known as the george washington of mexico because he helped to gain mexicos independence he had to fight against the spanish the french and the austrians in order to free his country

March 22

randolph caldecott was born on march 22 1846 he was born in chester england and beginned drawing when he was a young boy the caldecott medal is awarded each year to the illustrator of the most distinguished picture book

March 23

on march 23 1775 patrick henry gave a very famous speech in the speech, he said give me liberty, or give me death henry was a leader during the revolutionary war and encouraged the colonists to fight for independence from great britain

March 24

on march 24 1989 the exxon valdez ran aground in prince william sound off the coast of alaska the ship spilled almost 11 million gallons of oil many birds animals and fish were killed because they were covered in oil or ate fish covered in oil

March 25

gutzon borglum was born on march 25 1871 he is an american sculptor who is best knowed for carving mount rushmore in south dakota the memorial contains the heads of george washington thomas jefferson abraham lincoln and theodore roosevelt

March 26

robert frost was born on march 26 1874 he was a famous poet who wrote stopping by woods on a snowy evening robert did not attend school until he was 12 years old and never read a book until he was 14 he said every poem solves something for me in life

March 27

the strongest earth quake in american history shaked alaska on march 27 1964 it measured 9.2 on the richter scale and created a huge tsunami, or tidal wave, that killed 115 people

March 28

president george bush awarding the congressional gold medal to jesse owens on march 28 1990 owens winned for gold medals in track-and-field events in the 1936 olympics which were held in berlin germany

March 29

the first permanent white settlement in north america was established on march 29 1638 under the leadership of a man named peter minuit swedish settlers founded it the settlement was in what is now the state of delaware

March 30

vincent van gogh was born on march 30 1853 during his lifetime he only sold one of his painting, but they are worth millions today he said there is nothing in the world as interesting as people one can never study them enough

March 31

the eiffel tower was completed on march 31 1889 it was built by alexandre gustave eiffel and was the tallest building in the world at the time it is 985 feet high eiffel built the tower for the worlds fair in paris

April 1

april 1 is called april fools day it was first celebrated in france because the first day of spring and the new year both fell on april 1 even after the new year was change, some people still celebrated it and they were called "fools"

April 2

hans christian anderson was born on april 2 1805 he was a poet an author and a playwright but he is best knowed for his fairy tails he wrote the ugly duckling the emperors new clothes and the snow queen

April 3

jane goodall was born on april 3 1934 she is an expert on chimpanzees and has studied chimps in africa for over 30 years she is worryed about the survival of chimps and she is trying to find other solutions to live animal research

April 4

martin luther king, jr, was shot and killed on april 4 1968 in memphis tennessee king believed in non-violence but riots breaked out in many big citys after his death

April 5

booker t washington was born on april 5 1856 as a slave in virginia after becoming free, he went to School and later started the tuskegee institute he hoped blacks could gain equality threw education

April 6

matthew henson, an african american explorer, discovered the north pole on april 6 1909 henson made two earlier trips but had failed to reech the north pole finally, on his third try, he succeded robert peary and for eskimos accompanied him on this historic expedishun

on april 6 1896 the first modern olympic games were held in athens greece thirteen countrys came to the events some of the events included foot races discus throwing jumping and wrestling

April 7

april 7 is world health day every one is encouraged to eat healthy get enough sleep and exercise however, in poorer countries, doctors make sure that people have enough to eat and proper medical care

April 8

on april 8 1974 hank aaron hitted his 715th home run for the atlanta braves this home run breaked babe ruths record of 714 home runs aaron finished his career with 775 home runs

April 9

on april 9 1833 the first free public library opened in peterborough new hampshire sum of the taxs people pay are used for librarys a man named andrew carnegie donated 50 million dollars to build librarys in our country

April 10

the u.s. patent system was established on april 10 1790 some things that have been patented are the zipper the safety pin the toothpick and the eraser-tipped pencil

April 11

iowa became the first state to impose a cigarette tax on april 11 1921 this meaned that people had to pay extra for there cigarettes there is also a tax on alcohol why do you think the goverment taxs these kindz of items

on april 11 1968, one week after the assassination of martin luther king, jr, president lyndon johnson signed the civil rights act of 1968 into law one of the reasons for passing the law was to protect civil rights workers from violence

April 12

on april 12 1961 yuri gagarin becomed the first man in space he was from the soviet union and he made one orbit around the Earth aboard the spacecraft vostok I

April 13

thomas jefferson was born on april 13 1743 he was one of the authors of the declaration of independence and he was the third president he purchased the louisiana territory and helped plan the city of washington, d.c.

April 14

president abraham lincoln was assassinated on april 14 1865 by a man named john wilkes booth after booth shot lincoln at the ford's theatre, he jumped to the stage and breaked one of his legs lincoln died the next day in a house near the theater

April 15

leonardo da vinci was born on april 15 1452 he was a great painter sculptor and inventor he is most famous for his painting of the mona lisa in paris france

the titanic sinked on april 15 1912 after hitting an iceberg in the atlantic ocean more than 1500 people was killed because the ship didnt have enouf lifeboats in 1985 the ship was discovered on the ocean floor, sitting 2.5 miles below the waters surface

April 16

on april 16 1503 christopher columbus left veragua in central america to begin his trip back to europe this was his last voyage to america

April 17

the apollo 13 spacecraft landed safely in the pacific ocean on april 17 1970 during the mission, one of the oxygen tanks exploded and the astronauts were not sure they had enough energy to return to Earth one of the astronauts said houston, we have a problem

April 18

on april 18 1775 paul revere began his famous ride to warn the american colonists that the british were comeing he left boston massachusetts, at 10 pm and arrived in lexington at midnight to warn sam adams and john hancock

April 19

the battle of lexington and concord taked place on april 19 1775 this was the first battle of the american revolution why were americans fighting the british

April 20

adolf hitler was born on april 20 1889 he is known for being the leader of germany and the nazi party when he took over several countries in europe, world war II began he is responsible for the death of over six million jews in europe

April 21

a german educator named friedrich froebel was born on april 21 1782 he started the first kindergarten in 1837 the word kindergarten means "children's garden" the idea of kindergarten has since spread through out the world

April 22

the first earth day was celebrated on april 22 1970 twenty million americans participated in marches and rallies to protest pollution twenty years later, on april 22 1990, 200 million people participated in earth day in 141 different countries

April 23

william shakespeare was born on april 23 1564 he was a great english poet and playwright he writed romeo and juliet hamlet and macbeth

April 24

the first american league baseball game were played between cleveland and chicago on april 24 1901 chicago won by a score of 8 to 2 what two states are these citys in

April 25

on april 25 1901 new york becomed the first state to require automobile license plates it costed $1.00 to by the plates why do states require drivers to put license plates on theyre car

April 26

charles richter was born on april 26 1900 he was a seismologist who developed the richter scale this scale measures the force of earthquakes a quake of less then 3.0 is hardly noticeable but a quake of 6.0 can cause buildings to shake

April 27

ulysses s grant was born on april 27 1822 he was the eighteenth president of the united states he was also the commander of the union army during the civil war the transcontinental railroad was finished during his presidency

April 28

james monroe was born on april 28 1758 he was the fifth u.s. president and the only other president besides george washington to run unopposed what does unopposed mean

April 29

on april 29 1913 gideon sundback patented the zipper he called it a "separable fastener," because you could separate the too parts from each other and then fasten them back together again

April 30

on april 30 1803 napoleon sold the louisiana territory to president thomas jefferson for about 2 cents per acre it was the largest land purchase in world history what states were included in the louisiana territory

May 1

the empire state building was opened to the public on may 1 1931 it has 102 storys and is one of the taller buildings in the world the sears tower in chicago is now the tallest building in the united states

May 2

alaskas flag was adopted on may 2 1927 a seventh-grade student designing the flag alaska didnt never become a state until 1959 where could you find a picture of alaskas flag

May 3

golda meir was born on may 3 1898 she was born in russia but later moved to milwaukee wisconsin after she get marryed, she moved to palestine and worked for the government she eventually became the prime minister of israel

May 4

on may 4 1626 peter minuit landed on manhattan island and eventually buyed it for 24.00 from the native americans who were living there he payed for it with beads and trinkets

May 5

nellie bly was born on may 5 1867 she was the first female journalist to achieve world-wide fame she writed many storys about her courageous adventures and she traveled around the world in less then 80 days

May 6

the hindenburg a giant balloon-like vehicle exploded as it prepared to land in lakehurst new jersey, on may 6 1937 it had just finished a flight across the atlantic ocean it was filled with a very explosive gas called hydrogen

May 7

peter tchaikovsky was born on may 7 1840 he composed music and produced symphonys operas and ballets his ballets includes swan lake sleeping beauty and the nutcracker

May 8

harry s truman was was born on may 8 1884 he becamed our twenty-third president as president, he forsed the end of world war II by ordering the us military to drop atomic boms on the japanese cities of hiroshima and nagasaki

May 9

howard carter was born on may 9 1873 he discovered King Tut's tomb in egypt in 1922 king tuts tomb consisted of three rooms with couches food jewelry and boats inside.

May 10

on may 10 1869 the first transcontinental railroad was completed near promontory utah a golden spike was used to connect omaha nebraska, to sacramento california

May 11

minnesota became the thirty-second state on may 11 1858 it's state flower is the pink and white ladys slipper and the state bird is the common loon

May 12

florence nightingale was born on may 12 1820, in florence italy she nursed injured soldiers during wars and she is considered the founder of modern nursing

May 13

on may 13 1607 captain john smith and 105 colonists founded the jamestown colony in virginia this was the first permanent english settlement in america

May 14

gabriel daniel fahrenheit was born on may 14 1686 in 1714, he invented the type of thermometer that is used today the Fahrenheit temperature scale is named after him sum thermometer has a metrik temperature scale, which is named after someone else what is the name of the metrik temperature scale

May 15

L frank baum was born on may 15 1856 he wrote the book the wizard of oz and his story was later maked into a movie he also writted 13 other books about oz because people liked his first book so much

May 16

william seward was born on may 16 1801 he was the secretary of state and arranged for the purchase of alaska he runned against abraham lincoln for the republican nomination for president but losed he was also shot the same night as president lincoln but he survived

May 17

on may 17 1954 there was a very important supreme court decision it was called brown vs. board of education of topeka kansas and it sayed that separating blacks and whites in different schools were unfair and against the law

May 18

on may 18 1980 mt st helens erupted in the state of washington it is considered the worst volcanic disaster in the recorded history of the united states

May 19

malcolm x was born on may 19 1925 he leaded a black religious movement called the nation of black muslims many muslims used the letter X as a last name rather then the names given to they're ancestors bye slave owners. Malcolm X was shot while giving a speech in new york

May 20

on may 20 1932 amelia earhart began her famous flight across the atlantic ocean she was the first woman to fly alone across the atlantic during a later flight, she crashed and neither she nor her plane has ever been found

May 21

on may 21 1927 charles lindbergh finished his first solo flight across the atlantic ocean he flied from long island new york, to paris france, in his plain called the spirit of st louis the flight taked 33.5 hours

May 22

sir arthur conan doyle was born on may 22 1859 he was a british author and he writed mysterys about a character named sherlock holmes what is your favorite mystery

May 23

south carolina became the eighth state on may 23 1788 the state reptile is the loggerhead turtle the loggerheads make nests along the eastern coast of south carolina and are considered a threatened species

May 24

on may 24 1869 john wesley powell led the first expedition of the grand canyon he and nine men traveled by boat from the green river in wyoming to the colorado river, which has shaped the grand canyon

May 25

on may 25 1787 the constitutional convention opened in philadelphia pennsylvania with george washington as president many men comed to help write the constitution, which stated the laws for the united states

May 26

sally ride was born on may 26 1951 in june 1983, she was the first woman accepted
into the astronaut program she also became the first woman in space when she
traveled on the space shuttle challenger with four other astronauts

May 27

the golden gate bridge opened in san francisco on may 27 1937 it is one of the largest
and most spectacular suspension bridges in the world the brige is 8981 feet long and is
namd after the golden gate strait at the entrance to san francisco bay

May 28

jim thorpe was born on may 28 1886 he is one of the greatest athletes in history
he was born in prague oklahoma thorpe played major-league baseball professional
football and ran track and field

May 29

john f kennedy was born on may 29 1917, in brookline massachusetts he was the 35th
president and he fought for equal rights for african americans he was assassinated in
dallas texas, on november 22 1963

May 30

memorial day was first officially observed on may 30 1868 graves of american
soldiers are decorated with flowers on this day this holiday was first begun to honor
civil war veterans and is now observed on the last monday in may

May 31

walt whitman a famous american poet was born on may 31 1819 he wrote the poem O
Captain! My Captain! as a tribute to abraham lincoln he also cared for injured Union
soldiers during the civil war

June 1

happy birthday, kentucky and tennessee on june 1 1792 kentucky became the 15th state and on june 1 1796, tennessee becomed the 16th state tennessee later seceded during the civil war and was readmitted in 1866

June 2

martha dandridge was born on june 2 1731 after her furst husbund died martha married george washington martha washington was the furst furst lady of the united states

June 3

charles drew an african-american surgeon was born on june 3 1904 he discovered a way to store blood for transfusions, which saved many lives during world war II he quit his job to protest the separate storage of black and white people's blood

June 4

on june 4 1896 henry ford successfully test drived his first car on the streets of detroit michigan it was a horseless carriage called a Quadricycle

June 5

robert f kennedy was shot in a los angeles california, hotel on june 5 1968 he had just won the Democratic Presidential Primary in california he dyed the next day

June 6

british canadian and american troops invaded the beachs of normandy france, on june 6 1944 this invasion is known as D-Day and was very important because it lead to the end off world war II

June 7

on june 7 1776 richard henry lee of virginia proposed a declaration of independence to the continental congress he said these United Colonies are, and of right ought to be, free and independent states

June 8

frank lloyd wright was born on june 8 1867 he was a Famous architect who designed buildings that related in some way to their natural surroundings

June 9

george stephenson was born on june 9 1781 he is considerd the father of the railway system and he built a fast locomotive called Rocket that could carry passengers he didnt attend a formal school intil he was 19

June 10

on june 10 1928 maurice sendak was born he has writed more than 80 childrens books, but his most famous won is where the wild things are he has one the caldecott medal and the american book award

June 11

jacques cousteau was born in france on june 11 1910 he spent much of his life exploreing the oceans and he helped invent the SCUBA gear, which allows divers to breathe under water

June 12

anne frank was born on june 12 1929 she and her family hid from the nazis in holland during world war II they were eventually found by the germans and anne later died in a concentration camp her diary helped the world understand her familys story

June 13

president lyndon johnson appointed thurgood marshall to the united states supreme court on june 13 1967 he was the first african-american supreme court justice and he served until 1991

June 14

today is flag day on june 14 1777 the continental congress adopted the national flag they ruled that it should have thirteen red and white stripes and thirteen stars for the original thirteen colonies how many stars does the flag have now

June 15

on june 15 1752 benjamin franklin flew a kite during a thunder storm to prove that lightning carries a electric charge it is, in part, due to him that we have electric lights televisions and computers

June 16

valentina tereshkova became the first women in space on june 16 1963 she was from the soviet union and traveled around the Earth 45 times in three days she parachuted back to Earth after her spacecraft, the vostok 6, reentered the Earths atmosphere

June 17

five burglars were arrested breaking into the democratic party headquarters in the watergate hotel on june 17 1972 the crime and the attempt to cover it up were linked to president richard nixon he later resigned from office

June 18

the childrens book author and illustrator chris van allsburg was born on june 18 1949 he has won to caldecott medals and has wrote the books the polar express jumanji and just a dream

June 19

its juneteenth june 19 is a day on which many african americans celebrate the end of slavery on june 19 1865, Union soldiers landed at galveston texas they announced that the civil war was over and that all slaves were free

June 20

on june 20 1782 congress approved the Great Seal of the united states charles thomson redesined the seal after the continental congress rejected the first design, which was made by ben franklin, john adams, and thomas jefferson

June 21

on june 21 1788 new hampshire became the ninth state in the united states the constitution was officially adopted after new hamshire became the ninth state to ratify it

June 22

the 26th Amendment was signed on june 22 1970 this amendment changed the legal voting age from 21 to 18 how many years will it be until you are old enough to vote

June 23

wilma rudolph an african-american athelete was born on june 23 1940 she was the furst american to win three gold medals during one olympic games she had polio as a child and wore a steel brace for six years but she worked hard to succeed in basket ball and track

June 24

henry VIII was crowned king of england at the age of 18 on june 24 1509 he was very well educated and loved music and poetry but he was also extremely cruel and had two of his wifes beheaded

June 25

eric carle an author and illustrator of childrens books was born on june 25 1929 he has wrote and illustrated the very hungry caterpillar the very quiet cricket and the very grouchy lady bug

June 26

one of the greatest female athletes in history was born on june 26 1914 her name was "babe" didrikson zaharias she competed in swimming basketball golf and track and field

June 27

on june 27 1922 the first newbery medal was awarded to henrik van loon for his book the story of mankind the medal is awarded to the most distinguished childrens book published each year

June 28

on june 28 1894 congress made the first monday in september a national holiday the holiday was called labor day and was created to celebrate the contributions that workers make to our country

June 29

george washington goethals was born on june 29 1858 he was the chief engineer of the panama canal a passageway for ships that runs between north and south america before it was built, ships had to sail around the tip of south america

June 30

david mcPhail an author and illustrator of childrens books was born on june 30 1940 he often writes book about bears and one of his first books was the bears tooth ache he has written or illustrated over 40 books wow

JULY

July 1

diana spencer who later became the princess of wales was born on july 1 1961 she married prince charles in 1981 and they had two sons, william and henry princess diana was killed in a car accident in paris on august 30 1997

July 2

on july 2 1964 president lyndon johnson signed the civil rights act of 1964 this law banned discrimination because of a persons skin color religion gender or race

July 3

the battle of gettysburg ended on july 3 1863 it was fought in pennsylvania during the civil war and it was a victory for the union army of the north however, more than 45,000 lives were lost in the battle

July 4

on july 4 1776 the continental congress adopted the declaration of independence, which was written by thomas jefferson this document declared our independence from England and was signed by 56 men

July 5

phineas taylor barnum was born on july 5 1810 he started p.t. barnums traveling circus in 1870 he later asked james bailey to be his partner and they formed the barnum and bailey circus

July 6

the first all-star base ball game was played on july 6 1933 babe ruth hit the first home run in that game it was played at comiskey park in chicago illinois

July 7

on july 7 1981 president ronald reagan announced that he was nominating judge sandra day o'connor to the united states supreme cort she were the first female to become a supreme cort judge

July 8

on july 8 1776 the liberty bell was ringed to gather people so they could hear the declaration of independence red out loud there are many storys about how the bell cracked you can see the liberty bell in philadelphia pennsylvania

July 9

elias howe was born on july 9 1819 he was the inventor of the sewing machine tailors and seamstresses did not like the sewing machine because they thout they would be out of a job

July 10

mary mcLeod bethune was born on july 10 1875 she started a school for African-American girls in daytona florida, in 1904 the school later becomed bethune-cookman college mary also worked with four different presidents to improve the lifes of her peple

July 11

on july 11 1899 childrens book author e.b. white was born he lived on a farm in maine and often wrote about the animals that lived there can you name his most famous book about a pig and a spider

July 12

george eastman inventor of the Kodak camera was born on july 12 1854 he and william walker invented film that could be roled and advanced through a camera up until this time, photographers were useing a separate plate for each picture taken

July 13

father edward flanagan was born on july 13 1886 he was born in ireland and came to the united states to become a priest he later started boys town a caring home for troubled boys in omaha nebraska it is now called girls and boys town

July 14

gerald ford was born on july 14 1913, in omaha nebraska he was the 38th president of the united states and took over after richard nixon resigned from office

July 15

on july 15 1606 rembrandt was born in the netherlands he was a dutch painter who was famous for his use of light and shadow he painted many portraits and landscapes

July 16

the first atomic bomb was tested in a dessert in new mexico on july 16 1945 the explosion was equal to almost 20,000 tons of dynamite it created a 1200 foot crater in the ground

July 17

disneyland opened in anaheim california on july 17 1955 walt disney designed this amusement park disney theme parks have also opened in florida france and japan

July 18

john glenn was born on july 18 1921 he was the first american to orbit the Earth and one of the first astronauts in the space program he also became the oldest man to fly in space in 1998 at the age of 77

July 19

the first women's rights convention was held in seneca falls new york, on july 19 1848 elizabeth cady stanton and three other women meeted to demand equal rights for women, including the right to vote

July 20

on july 20 1969 buzz aldrin and neil armstrong became the first men to set foot on the moon armstrong said thats one small step for man, one giant step for mankind

July 21

the battle of bull run took place on july 21 1861 it was the first major battle of the civil war and was a victory for the south general jackson got the nickname "stonewall" as a result of this battle

July 22

alexander calder was born on july 22 1898 he was a sculptor who used mainly wire and metal in his artwork he is considerd to be the inventor of the mobile

July 23

ford motor company sold its first car on july 23 1903 the car was called a Model A henry ford started the company in june of 1903

July 24

on july 24 1847 brigham young and his followers arriveed in the valley of the great salt lake in utah they had traveled from illinois and were seeking a safe place to practice the Mormon religion

July 25

on july 25 1952 puerto rico became a self-governing commonwealth of the united states this means that puerto ricans follow some of the laws of the united states and they make some of there own laws to

July 26

new york became the 11th state to join the united states on july 26 1788 the state flower is the rose and the state muffin is the apple muffin what is the capital of new york

July 27

bugs bunny first appeared in a cartoon on july 27 1940 the cartoon was entitled a wild hare chuck jones created bugs bunny daffy duck porky pig and many other cartoon characters

July 28

beatrix potter the author of childrens books was born on july 28 1866 she grew up in london and had many pets most of the characters in her books are based on the pets she had as a child

July 29

charles william beebe a ocean explorer was born on july 29 1877 he and otis barton dived more than 3000 feet down in to the ocean in a steel ball called a bathysphere beebe was interested in finding new creatures that had never be seen before

July 30

on july 30 1863 henry ford was born in dearborn township michigan he started ford motor company and comed up with the idea to use an assembly line to make cars much faster this was called mass production

July 31

j.k. rowling was born on july 31 1965 she is the author of the harry potter series about a boy who attends the hogwarts school of witchcraft and wizardry

August 1

on august 1 1770 the explorer william clark was born he and meriweather lewis led an expedition to explore the western united states they drew maps of the land and kept journals of there travels to share with the american people

August 2

saddam hussein the leader of iraq ordered his army to invade kuwait on august 2 1990. president george bush sent u.s. troops to saudi arabia to help kuwait this action was called operation desert storm

August 3

on august 3 1610 english explorer henry hudson discovered a large bay on the east coast of canada he named it hudson bay he and his crew was looking for a passage to the pacific ocean

August 4

the u.s. coast guard was established on august 4 1790 it was created to enforce customs laws because the country was having problems with smuggling the coast guard is able to board and search any vessel in u.s. waters

August 5

neil armstrong was born on august 5 1930 he was the first person to walk on the moon he be the commander of the apollo 11 mission the other astronauts on board was buzz aldrin and mike collins

August 6

on august 6 1945 the united states dropped an atomic bomb on hiroshima japan, in an effort to end world war II the bomb killed nearly 140,000 people and was the first time a nuclear weapon had been used in war

August 7

on august 27 1927 the international peace bridge opened between buffalo new york and fort erie ontario it was dedicated to 100 years of friend ship between the u.s. and canada, the longest standing friend ship between two countrys that share a border

August 8

matthew henson was born on august 8 1866 he was an african-american explorer who was the first person to reach the north pole the leader of the expedition, robert peary, arrived 45 minutes later

August 9

the united states dropped a second atomic bomb on japan on august 9 1945 the bomb was dropped on the city of nagasaki and killed an estimated 74,000 people

August 10

on august 10 1846 congress chartered the smithsonian institution after james smithson gave $500,000 to set it up. the smithsonian institution is made up off 16 museums and galleries and the national zoo

August 11

joanna cole was born on august 11 1944 she and bruce degen have written the many books in the magic school bus series cole said writing is hard work, but its the greatest fun in the world

August 12

katherine lee bates was born on august 12 1859 she was the author and composer of the song america the beautiful the first line is oh, beautiful for spacious skies, for amber waves of grain

August 13

on august 13 1926 fidel castro the president of cuba was born he has been the communist leader of cuba since 1959, when he and his army took over this island country off the coast of florida

August 14

japan surrendered to the united states on august 14 1945 after the bombing of nagasaki and hiroshima, japanese emperor hirohito said we cannot continue the war any longer this ended world war II and is often called V-J day

August 15

on august 15 1769 napoleon bonaparte was born he was the emperor of france and the leader of the french revolution he was defeated by the british at the battle of waterloo and forced to give up his empire

August 16

matt christopher a childrens book author was born on august 16 1917 when matt was a child, him favorite sport was baseball as an adult, he wrote many books about sports

August 17

davy crockett was born on august 17 1786, in tennessee he was a congressman a soldier and a hunter he died fighting in the battle of the alamo in 1836

August 18

roberto clemente was born in puerto rico on august 18 1934 he were a base ball player for the pittsburgh pirates he died in a plane crash on december 31 1972, and was the first hispanic player to be inducted into the base ball hall of fame

August 19

on august 19 1871 orville wright was born orville and his brother wilbur invented and builded the first controlled air plane orville was the first to fly this plane and he stayd in the air four 12 seconds

August 20

vitus bering was choosed by peter the great to find a land connecting asia and north america there was no such land too be found but, on august 20 1741, he discovered alaska the bering strait and bering island are named after him

August 21

hawaii becomed the 50th state on august 21 1959 it was the last state to be admitted to the united states it is made up of ate main islands and it's capital is honolulu

August 22

on august 22 1864 twelve nations signed the geneva convention, witch established the red cross and made rules for how to treat wounded people and how to protect medical workers clara barton established the american red cross in 1881

August 23

on august 23 1775 king george III of england refused the american colonists' offers of peace and declared that the colonists were in rebellion the american revolution had all ready begun

August 24

mount vesuvius erupted on august 24 in AD 79 it destroyed the roman cities of pompeii and herculaneum around 20,000 people were killed in the eruption

August 25

on august 25 1916 the national park service was created within the Department Of The Interior there are approximately 380 national parks in the united states some of these include the grand canyon the washington monument and the everglades

August 26

the nineteenth amendment went into effect on august 26 1920 this amendment guaranteed women the write to vote it had first been introduced to congress in 1878

August 27

mother theresa was born on august 27 1910 she was a nun who pledged her life to helping the poor she were awarded the nobel peace prize and the medal of freedom for her work how old was she when she died on september 5 1997

August 28

on august 28 1963 martin luther king, jr, leaded the famous march on washington, d.c. he gave a speech to over 200,000 people from the steps of the lincoln memorial it were called i have a dream

August 29

francisco pizarro killed the incan king atahualpa on august 29 1533 pizarro and 200 spanish conquistadors had destroyed the incan civilization in search of gold in south america

August 30

donald crews the childrens book author and illustrator was borned on august 30 1938 he writted and illustrated ten black dots and freight train he often includes himself in his book illustrations

August 31

maria montessori was born on august 31 1870 she was unhappy with the way young children was educated so she began her own school she believed children could learn naturally thru they're environment

Septmeber 1

world war II beginned on september 1 1939, when adolf hitler and his german army invaded poland almost 40 million people was killed in this war

September 2

the great fire of london broke out on september 2 1666 within a few days, it had destroyed four-fifths of the city what country is london in

September 3

the united states and great britain sined the treaty of paris on september 3 1783 this treaty ended the american revolution and made the united states a free country

September 4

spanish settlers founded los angeles in what is now california on september 4 1781 it was originally named El Pueblo de Nuestra Senora la Reina de los Angeles, which means "The Town of Our Lady, the Queen of the Angels"

September 5

jesse james were born on september 5 1847, in kearney missouri he and a group of bandits spended there lifes robbing trains banks and stores they robbed their first train in 1873

September 6

on september 6 1941 all jews over the age of six that were living in german territories had to wear yellow stars of david on their cloths whenever they went out side

September 7

a very famous artist named grandma moses was born on september 7 1860 she didnt began painting until she was 78 years old but she lived to be 101

September 8

on september 8 1921 the first miss america was crowned her name was margaret gorman and she was only 15 years old some people think there shouldnt never be any more beauty pageants what do you think

September 9

california became the 31st state in the united states on september 9 1850 its capital is sacramento and it is known to have many earth quakes

September 10

elias howe patented his lockstitch sewing machine on september 10 1846 it sewed 250 stitchs a minute unfortunately, he couldnt get no one interested in buying it until much later

September 11

on september 11 2001 terrorists hijacked airplanes and flew them into the world trade center and the pentagon many people were killed, including firefighters and police officers. thank you're local firefighters and police officers today

September 12

the lascaux cave paintings were discovered in france by for teen agers and a dog on september 12 1940 the paintings are 17,000 years old and from the paleolithic period

September 13

on september 13 1788 congress authorized the first national election and selected new york city as the temporary capital of the united states what is the capital of the united states today

September 14

on september 14 1814 francis scott key wrote the star-spangled banner during the war of 1812 in 1931, president herbert hoover signed a bill making it the national anthem

September 15

tomie dePaola was born on september 15 1934 he is a childrens book author and illustrator who writes about his experiences as a children he won the caldecott honor award for his book entitled strega nona

September 16

the Pilgrims left england on the mayflower on september 16 1620 when they arrived in america, they settled in plymouth massachusetts they were seeking religious freedom

September 17

on september 17 1787 the men attending the constitutional convention signed the constitution of the united states this document set up are government and are laws

September 18

george washington laid the cornerstone of the u.s. capitol building in washington, d.c., on september 18 1793 members of congress meet in the capitol to discuss and make our countrys laws

September 19

jim abbott was born on september 19 1967, in flint michigan he was born without a right hand but became a major league baseball pitcher he also won a gold medal in the 1988 olympics, pitching for team usa

September 20

on september 20 1519 ferdinand magellan set sail from spain on a voyage around the world he was killed during the voyage but 18 men and one of his ships returned to spain this was the first circumnavigation of the globe

September 21

hurricane hugo hit charleston south carolina, on september 21 1989 a hurricane is a large rotating storm that forms over warm ocean waters hurricane season lasts from june thru november

September 22

president john kennedy signed an act that established the u.s. peace corps on september 22 1961 men and women join the peace corps to help people in other countries and to learn more about other cultures

September 23

on september 23 1846 johann galle discovered the planet neptune it is the eighth planet from the sun and takes 165 years two revolve around the sun

September 24

jim henson was born on september 24 1936 he was the creator of the muppets and sesame street he designed kermit the frog bert and ernie and many other muppets for these television shows

September 25

the explorer vasco nunez de balboa crossed a small strip of land known as panama on september 25 1513 he sighted the pacific ocean and claimed the ocean four spain

September 26

john chapman who was also knowed as johnny appleseed was born on september 26 1774 he traveled across pennsylvania ohio kentucky illinois and indiana planting apple trees

September 27

samuel adams was born on september 27 1722 he was an american patriot who helped to organize the boston tea party he also signed the declaration of independence and served as the governor of massachusetts

September 28

according to legend, on september 28 490 b1c, a greek soldier ran 26 miles from marathon to athens in greece to deliver a message that the greeks had defeated the persians this is how the word marathon came to be

September 29

the united states established the first regular army of 700 mans on september 29 1789 since this time, many men and women have gave their lifes for theyre country

September 30

on september 30 1861 william wrigley, jr., was born he was the founder of the wrigley chewing gum company and the owner of the chicago cubs baseball team wrigley field in chicago is named after him

October 1

on october 1 1971 walt disney world in orlando florida, opend then, on october 1 1982, epcot center opened at walt disney world at the epcot center, you can learn about energy dinosaurs plants and different countrys of the world

October 2

happy birthday, charlie brown the first peanuts comic strip appeared in news papers on october 2 1950 charles schulz created it the last peanuts comic strip appeared on february 13 2000

October 3

after world war II ended the berlin wall was constructed to divid germany into too kountries, east and west germany the two kountries were reunited on october 3 1990, when the wall was took down at that time the kountry resumed useing the original name germany

October 4

on october 4 1957 the soviet union launched the first man-made satellite into orbit it was called sputnik I and traveled around the Earth once every 96 minutes

October 5

chester arthur was borned on october 5 1830 he was the twenty-first president of the united states he becamed president after james garfield was shot and killed

October 6

on october 6 1927 the first full-length talking movie was released it was called the jazz singer and it starrd al jolson by 1930, movie studios were no longer making silent movies

October 7

desmond tutu was born on october 7 1931 he one the nobel peace prize and speaked out against apartheid in south africa apartheid is a system that has different laws for blacks and whites

October 8

the great chicago fire started on october 8 1871, and destroyed one-third of the city according to legend, the fire started when a cow in mrs o'learys barn kicked over a lantern

October 9

the washington monument opened to the public on october 9 1888 it was designed by robert mills and had elevators that carried visitors to the top in 12 minutes

October 10

on october 10 1942 james marshall the author of childrens books was born he writed the george and martha books and illustrated miss nelson is missing he created viola swamp after a real teacher he had

October 11

eleanor roosevelt was born on october 11 1884 she was the wife of president franklin roosevelt and traveled to europe during world war II as an ambassador of goodwill

October 12

on october 12 1492 christopher columbus seen an island in the bahamas that he named san salvador columbus was looking for a shortcut to asia and believed he had found one, but the bahamas is actually off the coast of north america

October 13

construction beginned on the white house on october 13 1792 george washington laid the cornerstone of the house but he didn't never actually get to live there who was the first president to live in the white house

October 14

on october 14 1912, while theodore roosevelt was campagneing for president, he was shooted in the chest the papers in his vest poket saved him and he insisted on finishing him speech before going to the hospitel

October 15

on october 15 1990 mikhail gorbachev won the nobel peace prize he was the president of the soviet union and helped to make the soviet union a more modern and democratic country

October 16

noah webster was born on october 16 1758 it took him 50 years to plan research and publish his american dictionary of the english language many people still use websters dictionarys today

October 17

on october 17 1989 the loma prieta earth quake hit san francisco california it occurred just minutes before the world series was going to start there and it caused $7 billion in damage

October 18

the united states flag was raised in alaska on october 18 1867 the u.s. had buyed alaska from russia for $7.2 million many people thought that was two expensive but they changed there minds when oil and gold was discovered there

October 19

on october 19 1860 an eleven-year-old girl named grace bedell wrote a letter to abraham lincoln who were running for president she tells him he wood look better with a beard, so he took her advise and grew one

October 20

herbert hoover died at the age of 90 on october 20 1964 he was the 31st president of the united states he was president during the economic depression of the 1930s

October 21

alfred nobel was born on october 21 1833 he invented dynamite and had 355 patents for his many inventions in his will, he leaved money to award nobel prizes to scientists writers and peacemakers,

October 22

general sam houston becomed the first president of the republic of texas on october 22 1836 this was before texas becomed a part of the united states there is a city in texas named for him

October 23

the famous brazilian soccer player named pele was born on october 23 1940 he played soccer for 22 years and scored 1281 goals during his career he encouraged many children all over the world to play soccer

October 24

on october 24 1901 a daring women named anna edson taylor rided inside a barrel over niagara falls during this adventure she falled 158 foots when rescuers got to anna, she said nobody ought ever do that again

October 25

richard byrd a famous antarctic explorer was born on october 25 1888 he was the first man to spend the winter exploring antarctica, the coldest place on Earth

October 26

on october 26 1825 the erie canal opened it was cutted through 363 miles of wilderness and was 40 feet wide it allowed ships to travel from new york to the midwest in order to trade goods

October 27

the first subway an under ground railway system began operating in new york city on october 27 1904 many people in new york still use the subway system as their mane form of transportation

October 28

the statue of liberty was a gift to are country from france it was so large it had to be shiped to the u.s. in peaces it was designed by frederic auguste bartholdi and was first unveiled in new york harbor on october 28 1886

October 29

on october 29 1929 the stock market crashed, causing people to sell 16 million shares of stock this was known as "black tuesday" and was the beginning of the great depression of the 1930s

October 30

john adams, are second president, was born on october 30 1735 he was one of the authors of the declaration of independence and he was the first president to live in the white house his sun, john quincy adams, becamed the sixth president.

October 31

the mount rushmore national monument was completed on october 31 1941 it is located in south dakota which four presidents did gutzon borglum carv into the monument

November 1

on november 1 1800 the white house became the official home of all u.s. presidents john and abigail adams moved into the house even though it was not quiet finished

November 2

daniel boone was born on november 2 1734 as an adult, he traveled from north carolina to kentucky which was an unsettled area he paved the way for thousands of pioneers to move to kentucky

November 3

on november 3 1957 a dog named laika becomed the worlds first space traveler the dog were on board a soviet satellite called sputnik II

November 4

iranian students who were followers of the ayatollah khomeini seized the u.s. embassy in tehran iran, on november 4 1979 they held 52 americans hostage for 444 days

November 5

on november 5 1872 susan b. anthony was arrested and fined $100.00 for trying to vote in a presidential election she was released from prison but never paid the fine she continued to work for the right to vote for women

November 6

adolphe sax was born on november 6 1814 he maked musical instruments and was from bulgaria he invented a famous instrument what instrument did he invent

November 7

franklin delano roosevelt became the first president to be reelected for a fourth term on november 7 1944 now presidents are only allowed to be reelected for too terms

November 8

montana became the 41st state to join the united states on november 8 1889 the capital of montana is helena part of which national park is located in montana

November 9

on november 9 1938 nazi soldiers destroyed jewish synagogues businesses and homes in what became known as Kristallnacht, which means "Crystal Night" the soldiers sended 30,000 jews to concentration camps

November 10

the television show sesame street was shown on public television for the first time on november 10 1969 it starred big bird oscar the grouch and cookie monster

November 11

november 11 is veterans day it is a day to honor all of those who has fighted in wars for are country. It is celebrated on November 11 because the peace treaty ending world war I was signed on this day in 1918

November 12

on november 12 1954 ellis island in new york harbor closed this island had being used since 1892 to process 20 million immigrants as they entered the united states

November 13

the vietnam veterans memorial was dedicated in washington, d.c., on november 13 1982 the memorial was designed by maya ying lin and is a long, polished, black wall that lists the names of soldiers killed or missing in the vietnam war

November 14

on november 14 1907 childrens book author william steig was born he didnt begin writing until he is 60 years old his most famouser book is sylvester and the magic pebble

November 15

the continental congress adopted the articles of confederation on november 15 1777 this document united the 13 colonies and led to the writing of the u.s. constitution

November 16

indian territory and oklahoma territory were combined and oklahoma becomed the 46th state on november 16 1907 what is the capital of oklahoma

November 17

the suez canal opened in egypt on november 17 1869 it connected the mediterranean sea with the red sea the canal made it much easier for ships to reach the middle east and asia, with out having to sail around africa

November 18

happy birthday, mickey mouse on november 18 1928 mickey mouse was first sawed in a black-and-white cartoon called steamboat willie walt disney got the idea for mickey from two real mouses that scampered across his drawing board

November 19

james garfield our 20th president was born on november 19 1831, in orange ohio before he became president, he worked as a janitor teacher preacher and general he was shot and killed while he was president

November 20

african-american inventor garrett morgan received a patent for the traffic light on november 20 1923 he invented it after seeing a accident between a carriage and a car in what order are the lights on a traffic light

November 21

on november 21 1620 the men on the mayflower signed the mayflower compact this was an agreement that they would rule theirselves and not be ruled by no king

November 22

lee harvey oswald assassinnated president john f. kennedy on november 22, 1963, in dallas, texas there has always been a lot of controversy surrounding Kennedys death

November 23

franklin pierce was born on november 23 1804 he were the 14th president of the united states the north and the south were becoming divided over the issue of slavery during his presidency

November 24

a very famous jazz pianist and composer named scott joplin was born on november 24 1868 he wrote the entertainer and maple leaf rag his music was not recorded untl after his death

November 25

childrens book author and illustrator marc brown was born on november 25 1946 he wrote books about arthur the anteater, his famousest character in marcs storys arthur even has his own television show

November 26

on november 26 1863 president abraham lincoln proclaimed that thanksgiving should be celebrated every year on the last thursday in november sarah josepha hale persuaded lincoln to make thanksgiving a national holiday

November 27

kevin henkes was born on november 27 1960 he writes and illustrates books for children he has writed lillys purple plastic purse chrysanthemum and owen

November 28

on november 28 1895 j frank duryea won the first u.s. auto race between gasoline-powered automobiles duryeas average speed was 7.5 miles per hour and he won $2000.00

November 29

louisa may alcott was born on november 29 1832 she wrote a very famous book entitled little women many of the storys in the book are based on her life this book was later made into a movie

November 30

samuel clemens, who is better knowed as mark twain, was born in florida missouri, on november 30 1835 he was a reporter during the civil war and later wrote famous books such as tom sawyer and huckleberry finn

December 1

on december 1 1955 an african-american woman named rosa parks was arrested because she wouldnt give up her seat on a city bus to a white person african americans in montgomery alabama, decided to boycott the buses until they were treated fairly

December 2

david macaulay was born on december 2 1946 he is a childrens book author and illustrator who has all ways been interested in the way things work some of his books our cathedral, city, and pyramid

December 3

illinois became the 21st state on december 3 1818 it has the sixth higher state population in the united states its largest city is chicago but the capital is springfield

December 4

wassily kandinsky was born on december 4 1866 he were a russian artist and he is considered the first abstract painter abstract art is the opposite of realistic art

December 5

happy birthday walt disney disney was born on december 5 1901, in chicago illinois he studied art and moved to hollywood to make movies such as mary poppins peter pan and fantasia

December 6

on december 6 1941 franklin delano roosevelt made a personal appeal for peace to emperor hirohito of japan roosevelt was trying to keep the united states out of world war II

December 7

japanese bombers launched a surprise attack on pearl harbor in hawaii on december 7 1941 in the attack the japanese sank 18 ships, destroyed 200 planes, and killed 3700 people president roosevelt said it is a day that will live in infamy

December 8

the united states entered world war II on december 8 1941 congress declared war on japan one day after the attack on pearl harbor the u.s. later entered the war in europe also

December 9

roller skates were patented on december 9 1884 they was first invented in holland but they were patented in the united states the first roller skates was very similar to today's rollerblades

December 10

melvil dewey was born on december 10 1851 he was an american librarian and he invented the dewey decimal system this is the number system used to classify non-fiction bookes

December 11

on december 11 1816 indiana becomed the 19th state there is a very famous car race holded in indianas capital city what is the name of this race

December 12

guglielmo marconi received the first transatlantic radio signal on december 12 1901 he had been experimenting with radio waves since 1895 and he later opend the first wireless telegraph service

December 13

on december 13 1642 the dutch navigator and explorer abel janszoon tasman discovered new zealand the country of tasmania and the animal known as the tasmanian devil are named after him

December 14

on december 14 1911 the dutch explorer roald amundsen was the first man to reach the south pole he went on this expedition after he losed the race to the north pole to matthew henson and robert peary

December 15

u.s. soldiers killed sitting bull in south dakota on december 15 1890 Sitting Bull was a famous sioux chief who did not want to live on a reservation, which is a place where native americans was forced to live after white settlers took there land

December 16

the boston tea party taked place on december 16 1773 american colonists was upset because the king of england was taxing them for tea and other items them protested by dressing up as indians and dumping a shipload full of tea into boston harbor

December 17

on december 17 1944 the united states ended the internment of japanese americans after the attack on pearl harbor, the u.s. government removed many japanese americans from their homes on the west coast and forced them to live in internment camps

December 18

the u.s. congress adopted the thirteenth amendment on december 18 1865 this amendment officially ended slavery after the civil war

December 19

on december 19 1843 charles dickens published his book entitled a chirstmas carol in this story, a man named scrooge learns the true meaning of christmas after bein visited by ghosts from the past present and future

December 20

south carolina becomed the first state to secede from the united states on december 20 1860 ten other states later seceded they formed their own country called the confederate states of america and elected jefferson davis as their president this led to the civil war

December 21

after a very long journey from england, the pilgrims landed at plymouth massachusetts, on december 21 1620, they had been sailing on the mayflower for over three months

December 22

the continental congress established the continental navy on december 22 1775 esek hopkins was made commander of the navy, which consisted of seven ships

December 23

on december 23 1823 the famous poem, a visit from st. nicholas, was first published written clement c. moore wrote the poem the first line is 'twas the night before christmas....

December 24

the united states and great britain signed a peace treaty that ended the war of 1812 on december 24 1814 in this treaty, the u.s. and great britain pledged to put a end to the atlantic slave trade

December 25

christmas is the festival celebrateing the birth of jesus christ and is observed by christians in most countrys on december 25 some traditions associated with this holiday are decorating ever green tree and hanging stockings

December 26

december 26 is the first day of kwanzaa african americans celebrate kwanzaa by lighting a candle each day until january 1 each candle represents a kwanzaa principle like unity and faith

December 27

another holiday that is celebrated at this time of year is hanukkah, a jewish holiday that lasts for eight days jewish people light a candle on the menorah for each of the eight days the dates for this holiday change every year in some years it is on this date

December 28

iowa becomed the 29th state to be admitted to the union on december 28 1846 iowa is bordered by both the missouri river and the mississippi river what is the capital of iowa

December 29

president andrew johnson was born on december 29 1808, in a two-room shack in north carolina he took over as president after abraham lincoln was assassinated

December 30

childrens book author and illustrator mercer mayer was born on december 30 1943 he has wrote over 300 books but he is most famous for his little critter books

December 31

on december 31 1907 the first ball was lowered at times square to celebrate the new year it has been a tradition ever since the ball is made of waterford crystal and weighs about 1,070 pounds

Web Sites

The Web sites below and on the following pages may be used as an extension activity to allow students to learn more about the events in history that occurred during each month. At the beginning of each month, bookmark the appropriate sites so students can explore them throughout the month. Care has been taken to find Web sites that are of good quality, as well as enduring and consistent. However, Web sites can change their URLs, undergo technical difficulties, or be incompatible with certain browsers. For this reason, there are several key words listed at the bottom of the page for each month (pages 68-78). You can utilize these words to conduct an Internet search of your own. Child-friendly search engines are listed below.

Every school should have an appropriate use policy regarding technology and the Internet, but, as with all classroom content, you are responsible for monitoring what your students are searching for and viewing on the Internet. It is always recommended that you preview a site before bookmarking it or recommending it to students.

It is also recommended that you discuss aspects of critical literacy with your students. Students should understand that anyone can publish information and opinions on the Internet. Students should be taught to look for the source of the information and evaluate it for any bias. For example, search results using the key word smoking may display a site from a cigarette company and a site from the U.S. Surgeon General's Office. Obviously, these two sites will have very different information and students need to be taught how to evaluate that information and look for biases.

Child-Friendly Search Engines

Yahooligans

　　http://www.yahooligans.com

KidsClick! Web Search for Kids by Librarians

　　http://sunsite.berkeley.edu/KidsClick!/

Site for Biographies of U.S. Presidents: White House

　　http://www.whitehouse.gov/history/presidents/

National Women's Hall of Fame

　　http://www.greatwomen.org/

Web Sites

Emancipation Proclamation at the National Archives
> Go to *http://www.teachercreated.com/books/3051*
> Click on page 68, site 1

Alaska for Kids Web Site
> Go to *http://www.teachercreated.com/books/3051*
> Click on page 68, site 2

United Nations Home Page
> Go to *http://www.teachercreated.com/books/3051*
> Click on page 68, site 3

Virtual Office of the Surgeon General
> Go to *http://www.teachercreated.com/books/3051*
> Click on page 68, site 4

Online Fairy Tales
> Go to *http://www.teachercreated.com/books/3051*
> Click on page 68, site 5

Paddington Bear Official Web Site
> Go to *http://www.teachercreated.com/books/3051*
> Click on page 68, site 6

Martin Luther King, Jr.
> Go to *http://www.teachercreated.com/books/3051*
> Click on page 68, site 7

The Inaugural Classroom
> Go to *http://www.teachercreated.com/books/3051*
> Click on page 68, site 8

Official Site of the National Football League
> Go to *http://www.teachercreated.com/books/3051*
> Click on page 68, site 9

Colonial Hall: A Look at America's Founders
> Go to *http://www.teachercreated.com/books/3051*
> Click on page 68, site 10

Key Words

- Alaska
- Australia
- Battle of New Orleans
- Benjamin Franklin
- Carl Sandburg
- Confederate Army
- Czar Nicholas II
- Emancipation Proclamation
- Fairy Tales
- Founding Fathers
- Franklin D. Roosevelt
- Franz Peter Schubert
- Inauguration
- James Cook
- John F. Kennedy
- John Hancock
- John Sutter
- Louis Braille
- Martin Luther King, Jr.
- NASA
- National Football League
- Olympics
- Postage Stamps
- Revolutionary War
- Richard Nixon
- Robert E. Lee
- United Nations
- William McKinley
- Winter Olympics

Web Sites

The Official Web Site of the Punxsutawney Groundhog Club

> Go to *http://www.teachercreated.com/books/3051*
> Click on page 69, site 1

Babe Ruth: The Official Web Site of the Sultan of Swat

> Go to *http://www.teachercreated.com/books/3051*
> Click on page 69, site 2

Exploring the Planets

> Go to *http://www.teachercreated.com/books/3051*
> Click on page 69, site 3

The Internet African American History Challenge

> Go to *http://www.teachercreated.com/books/3051*
> Click on page 69, site 4

The Alamo

> Go to *http://www.teachercreated.com/books/3051*
> Click on page 69, site 5

Grimm's Fairy Tales: From Folklore to Forever

> Go to *http://www.teachercreated.com/books/3051*
> Click on page 69, site 6

Gold Rush: California's Untold Stories

> Go to *http://www.teachercreated.com/books/3051*
> Click on page 69, site 7

Ancient Egypt: Online at the Rom

> Go to *http://www.teachercreated.com/books/3051*
> Click on page 69, site 8

Key Words

- Abraham Lincoln
- African-American History
- Alamo
- Alan Shepard
- Amelia Earhart
- Ancient Egypt
- Babe Ruth
- Charles Lindbergh
- Clyde Tombaugh
- Elizabeth Blackwell
- Frederick Douglass
- Galileo Galilei
- George Washington
- Gettysburg Address
- Groundhog Day
- Jules Verne
- King Tut
- Langston Hughes
- Laura Ingalls Wilder
- Marian Anderson
- Mark Spitz
- Planets
- Pyramids
- Solar System
- Thomas Edison
- Valentine's Day
- Washington Monument
- Wilhelm Grimm
- William Henry Harrison

Web Sites

Nebraska State Capital Virtual tour
> Go to *http://www.teachercreated.com/books/3051*
> Click on page 70, site 1

Dr. Seuss's Seussville
> Go to *http://www.teachercreated.com/books/3051*
> Click on page 70, site 2

Pasadena Kid's Page: Alexander Graham Bell
> Go to *http://www.teachercreated.com/books/3051*
> Click on page 70, site 3

National Geographic: The Underground Railroad
> Go to *http://www.teachercreated.com/books/3051*
> Click on page 70, site 4

Visit With Juliette Gordon Low
> Go to *http://www.teachercreated.com/books/3051*
> Click on page 70, site 5

A Virtual Journey into the Universe
> Go to *http://www.teachercreated.com/books/3051*
> Click on page 70, site 6

National Geographic: Discovering Mexico
> Go to *http://www.teachercreated.com/books/3051*
> Click on page 70, site 7

Caldecott Medal Home Page
> Go to *http://www.teachercreated.com/books/3051*
> Click on page 70, site 8

Legacy of an Oil Spill: Ten Years After Exxon Valdez
> Go to *http://www.teachercreated.com/books/3051*
> Click on page 70, site 9

Official Site of the Eiffel Tower (Note: the site is in French)
> Go to *http://www.teachercreated.com/books/3051*
> Click on page 70, site 10

Key Words

- Albert Einstein
- Alexander Graham Bell
- Amerigo Vespucci
- Atom Bomb
- Benito Juarez
- Boston Massacre
- Caldecott Medal
- Charles B. Darrow
- Dr. Seuss
- Earthquake

- Eiffel Tower
- Exxon Valdez
- Girl Scouts
- Grover Cleveland
- Gutzon Borglum
- Harriet Tubman
- International Women's Day
- Juliette Gordon
- Julius Caesar
- Knute Rockne

- Michelangelo
- Monopoly
- Nebraska
- Randolph Caldecott
- St. Patrick's Day
- Underground Railroad
- Universe
- Uranus
- William Herschel
- Women's Hall of Fame

Web Sites

The Jane Goodall Institute

> Go to *http://www.teachercreated.com/books/3051*
> Click on page 71, site 1

Exploratorium: The Science of Baseball

> Go to *http://www.teachercreated.com/books/3051*
> Click on page 71, site 2

U.S. Patent and Trademark Office Kid's Page

> Go to *http://www.teachercreated.com/books/3051*
> Click on page 71, site 3

Monticello: The Home of Thomas Jefferson

> Go to *http://www.teachercreated.com/books/3051*
> Click on page 71, site 4

Exploring Leonardo

> Go to *http://www.teachercreated.com/books/3051*
> Click on page 71, site 5

The Apollo Program: Apollo 13

> Go to *http://www.teachercreated.com/books/3051*
> Click on page 71, site 6

Liberty: The American Revolution

> Go to *http://www.teachercreated.com/books/3051*
> Click on page 71, site 7

American Experience: Adolf Hitler

> Go to *http://www.teachercreated.com/books/3051*
> Click on page 71, site 8

The Official Site of Major League Baseball

> Go to *http://www.teachercreated.com/books/3051*
> Click on page 71, site 9

Key Words

- Adolf Hitler
- American Revolution
- Apollo 13
- April Fools Day
- Baseball
- Booker T. Washington
- Christopher Columbus
- Earth Day
- Ford Theatre
- Germany
- Hank Aaron
- Hans Christian Anderson
- Jane Goodall
- John Wilkes Booth
- Leonardo daVinci
- Louisiana Territory
- Major Baseball League
- Martin Luther King, Jr.
- Matthew Henson
- Monticello
- NASA
- North Pole
- Olympics
- Paul Revere
- Robert Peary
- Thomas Jefferson
- Titanic
- William Shakespeare
- World Health Day
- Yuri Gagarin

Web Sites

50 States.com
> Go to *http://www.teachercreated.com/books/3051*
> Click on page 72, site 1

The American Experience: Around the World in 72 Days
> Go to *http://www.teachercreated.com/books/3051*
> Click on page 72, site 2

The Classical Archives: Tchaikovsky
> Go to *http://www.teachercreated.com/books/3051*
> Click on page 72, site 3

PBS: Secrets of the Pharaohs
> Go to *http://www.teachercreated.com/books/3051*
> Click on page 72, site 4

Brown vs. Board of Education: The Interactive Experience
> Go to *http://www.teachercreated.com/books/3051*
> Click on page 72, site 5

Eruptions of Mount St. Helens: Page and Present and Future
> Go to *http://www.teachercreated.com/books/3051*
> Click on page 72, site 6

Sherlock Holmes Museum: The World's Most Famous Address
> Go to *http://www.teachercreated.com/books/3051*
> Click on page 72, site 7

The American Experience: Lost in the Grand Canyon
> Go to *http://www.teachercreated.com/books/3051*
> Click on page 72, site 8

Founding Fathers: Delegates to the Constitutional Convention
> Go to *http://www.teachercreated.com/books/3051*
> Click on page 72, site 9

Exploratorium Golden Gate Bridge Cam
> Go to *http://www.teachercreated.com/books/3051*
> Click on page 72, site 10

Key Words

- Alaska
- Amelia Earhart
- Constitutional Convention
- Empire State Building
- Founding Fathers
- Gabriel Daniel Fahrenheit
- Golda Meir
- Golden Gate Bridge
- Grand Canyon
- Harry S. Truman
- Hindenburg
- Howard Carter
- Islam
- Jamestown
- John Wesley Powell
- King Tut
- Malcolm X
- Memorial Day
- Minnesota
- Mount St. Helens
- Nellie Bly
- Peter Minuit
- Peter Tchaikovsky
- Pharaohs
- San Francisco
- Sherlock Holmes
- Supreme Court
- Transcontinental Railroad
- William Seward
- World War II

Web Sites

Robert F. Kennedy Memorial
> Go to *http://www.teachercreated.com/books/3051*
> Click on page 73, site 1

Frank Lloyd Wright
> Go to *http://www.teachercreated.com/books/3051*
> Click on page 73, site 2

The Cousteau Society: Dolphin Log
> Go to *http://www.teachercreated.com/books/3051*
> Click on page 73, site 3

Anne Frank Center USA Website
> Go to *http://www.teachercreated.com/books/3051*
> Click on page 73, site 4

Energy Quest
> Go to *http://www.teachercreated.com/books/3051*
> Click on page 73, site 5

The New Hampshire Almanac
> Go to *http://www.teachercreated.com/books/3051*
> Click on page 73, site 6

Tudors and Henry VIII
> Go to *http://www.teachercreated.com/books/3051*
> Click on page 73, site 7

Official Eric Carle Web Site
> Go to *http://www.teachercreated.com/books/3051*
> Click on page 73, site 8

Newbery Medal Home Page
> Go to *http://www.teachercreated.com/books/3051*
> Click on page 73, site 9

The Panama Canal
> Go to *http://www.teachercreated.com/books/3051*
> Click on page 73, site 10

Flag of the United States
> Go to *http://www.teachercreated.com/books/3051*
> Click on page 73, site 11

Key Words

- Anne Frank
- Benjamin Franklin
- Charles Drew
- Continental Congress
- D-Day
- Declaration of Independence
- Dolphins
- Eric Carle
- Flag Day
- Frank Lloyd Wright
- George Stephenson
- Henry Ford
- Henry VIII
- Jacques Cousteau
- Juneteenth
- Kentucky
- Labor Day
- Martha Washington
- Maurice Sendak
- Memorial Day
- New Hampshire
- Newbery Medal
- Panama Canal
- Richard Henry Lee
- Tennessee
- Thurgood Marshall
- Tudors
- Valentina Tereshkova
- Watergate
- Wilma Rudolph

Web Sites

Ringling Brothers and Barnum & Bailey Online

> Go to *http://www.teachercreated.com/books/3051*
> Click on page 74, site 1

Liberty Bell

> Go to *http://www.teachercreated.com/books/3051*
> Click on page 74, site 2

The Wizard of Photography

> Go to *http://www.teachercreated.com/books/3051*
> Click on page 74, site 3

Girls and Boys Town

> Go to *http://www.teachercreated.com/books/3051*
> Click on page 74, site 4

John Glenn Orbits the Earth

> Go to *http://www.teachercreated.com/books/3051*
> Click on page 74, site 5

Welcome to Puerto Rico

> Go to *http://www.teachercreated.com/books/3051*
> Click on page 74, site 6

Official Site of Chuck Jones

> Go to *http://www.teachercreated.com/books/3051*
> Click on page 74, site 7

The Peter Rabbit Official Web Site

> Go to *http://www.teachercreated.com/books/3051*
> Click on page 74, site 8

Key Words

- American Civil War
- Apollo 11
- Barnum and Bailey Circus
- Battle of Bull Run
- Battle of Gettysburg
- Beatrix Potter
- Charles William Beebe
- Chuck Jones
- Declaration of Independence
- Disneyland

- E.B. White
- Father Edward Flanagan
- George Eastman
- Gerald Ford
- Gettysburg
- Girls and Boys Town
- Harry Potter
- Henry Ford
- John Glenn
- Liberty Bell

- Lyndon Johnson
- Mary McLeod Bethune
- Mormon
- Neil Armstrong
- New York
- Peter Rabbit
- Photography
- Princess Diana
- Puerto Rico
- Thomas Jefferson

Web Sites

Lewis & Clark Online Base Camp
    Go to http://www.teachercreated.com/books/3051
    Click on page 75, site 1

U.S. Coast Guard: Kid's Corner
    Go to http://www.teachercreated.com/books/3051
    Click on page 75, site 2

Hiroshima: A Survivor's Story
    Go to http://www.teachercreated.com/books/3051
    Click on page 75, site 3

Scholastic's: The Magic School Bus
    Go to http://www.teachercreated.com/books/3051
    Click on page 75, site 4

Napoleon
    Go to http://www.teachercreated.com/books/3051
    Click on page 75, site 5

National Baseball Hall of Fame: Roberto Clemente
    Go to http://www.teachercreated.com/books/3051
    Click on page 75, site 6

Hawaii State Government
    Go to http://www.teachercreated.com/books/3051
    Click on page 75, site 7

The National Park Service: ParnNet
    Go to http://www.teachercreated.com/books/3051
    Click on page 75, site 8

Mother Teresa: Angel of Mercy
    Go to http://www.teachercreated.com/books/3051
    Click on page 75, site 9

Conquistadors: The Conquest of the Incas
    Go to http://www.teachercreated.com/books/3051
    Click on page 75, site 10

Key Words

- Atomic Bomb
- Conquistadors
- Cuba
- Davy Crockett
- Fidel Castro
- Francisco Pizarro
- Geneva Convention
- Hawaii
- Henry Hudson
- Hiroshima
- International Peace Bridge
- Iraq
- Japanese Surrender
- Joanna Cole
- King George III
- Lewis & Clark Expedition
- Matthew Henson
- Mother Theresa
- Mount Vesuvius
- Napoleon Bonaparte
- National Parks
- Neil Armstrong
- Nineteenth Amendment
- Operation Desert Storm
- Red Cross
- Roberto Clemente
- Smithsonian Institution
- U.S. Coast Guard
- World War II
- Wright Brothers

Web Sites

World War II: Guts and Glory

> Go to *http://www.teachercreated.com/books/3051*
> Click on page 76, site 1

United States Holocaust Memorial Museum

> Go to *http://www.teachercreated.com/books/3051*
> Click on page 76, site 2

The Cave of Lascaux

> Go to *http://www.teachercreated.com/books/3051*
> Click on page 76, site 3

Virtual Tour of Plimouth Plantation

> Go to *http://www.teachercreated.com/books/3051*
> Click on page 76, site 4

U.S. Capitol Virtual Tour: A "Capitol" Experience

> Go to *http://www.teachercreated.com/books/3051*
> Click on page 76, site 5

Hyper Hurricanes

> Go to *http://www.teachercreated.com/books/3051*
> Click on page 76, site 6

Peace Corps Kids World

> Go to *http://www.teachercreated.com/books/3051*
> Click on page 76, site 7

National Geographic: Virtual Solar System

> Go to *http://www.teachercreated.com/books/3051*
> Click on page 76, site 8

Jim Henson Company

> Go to *http://www.teachercreated.com/books/3051*
> Click on page 76, site 9

Key Words

- Beauty Pageants
- California
- Earthquakes
- Ferdinand Magellan
- Frances Scott Key
- Grandma Moses
- Great London Fire
- Holocaust
- Hurricanes
- Jesse James
- Jim Henson
- Johnny Appleseed
- Lascaux Cave Paintings
- Los Angeles
- Major League Baseball
- Mayflower
- National Election
- Neptune
- Peace Corps
- Pilgrims
- Plimouth Plantation
- Samuel Adams
- Sewing Machine
- Solar System
- Treaty of Paris
- U.S. Capitol
- Vasco Nunez de Balboa
- Washington, D.C.
- William Wrigley, Jr.
- World War II

Web Sites

Walt Disney World

> Go to *http://www.teachercreated.com/books/3051*
> Click on page 77, site 1

The Official Peanuts Web Site

> Go to *http://www.teachercreated.com/books/3051*
> Click on page 77, site 2

Chicago Fire!

> Go to *http://www.teachercreated.com/books/3051*
> Click on page 77, site 3

The White House

> Go to *http://www.teachercreated.com/books/3051*
> Click on page 77, site 4

Alaska: The Great Land

> Go to *http://www.teachercreated.com/books/3051*
> Click on page 77, site 5

Nobel e- Museum

> Go to *http://www.teachercreated.com/books/3051*
> Click on page 77, site 6

SeaLab: Antartica

> Go to *http://www.teachercreated.com/books/3051*
> Click on page 77, site 7

New York Underground

> Go to *http://www.teachercreated.com/books/3051*
> Click on page 77, site 8

Mount Rushmore

> Go to *http://www.teachercreated.com/books/3051*
> Click on page 77, site 9

Key Words

- Al Jolson
- Alaska
- Alfred Nobel
- Antarctica
- Berlin Wall
- Charles Schultz
- Charlie Brown
- Chester Arthur
- Christopher Columbus
- Declaration of Independence
- Desmond Tutu
- Disney World
- Eleanor Roosevelt
- Erie Canal
- Great Chicago Fire
- Great Depression
- Houston
- Mikhail Gorbachev
- Mount Rushmore
- Noah Webster
- Nobel Prize
- Pele
- Republic of Texas
- Soccer
- Sputnik I
- Statue of Liberty
- Theodore Roosevelt
- Walt Disney
- Washington Monument
- White House

Web Sites

National Geographic's Inside the White House
  Go to *http://www.teachercreated.com/books/3051*
  Click on page 78, site 1

Veteran's Day
  Go to *http://www.teachercreated.com/books/3051*
  Click on page 78, site 2

American Family Immigration History Center: Explore Your Family History at Ellis Island
  Go to *http://www.teachercreated.com/books/3051*
  Click on page 78, site 3

State of Oklahoma
  Go to *http://www.teachercreated.com/books/3051*
  Click on page 78, site 4

The Sixth Floor Museum at Dealy Plaza
  Go to *http://www.teachercreated.com/books/3051*
  Click on page 78, site 5

The First Thanksgiving
  Go to *http://www.teachercreated.com/books/3051*
  Click on page 78, site 6

Kevin Henkes
  Go to *http://www.teachercreated.com/books/3051*
  Click on page 78, site 7

Orchard House: Home of the Alcotts
  Go to *http://www.teachercreated.com/books/3051*
  Click on page 78, site 8

The Mark Twain House
  Go to *http://www.teachercreated.com/books/3051*
  Click on page 78, site 9

Vietnam Veterans Memorial
  Go to *http://www.teachercreated.com/books/3051*
  Click on page 78, site 10

Key Words

- Abigail Adams
- Abraham Lincoln
- Articles of Confederation
- Ayatollah Khomeini
- Continental Congress
- Daniel Boone
- Ellis Island
- Garrett Morgan
- Immigrants
- John Adams

- John F. Kennedy
- Kevin Henkes
- Laika
- Lee Harvey Oswald
- Louisa May Alcott
- Mark Twain
- Montana
- Nazis
- Oklahoma
- Saxaphone

- Scott Joplin
- Slavery
- *Sputnik II*
- Suez Canal
- Susan B. Anthony
- Thanksgiving
- Veterans Day
- Vietnam Veterans Memorial
- Vietnam War
- White House

Web Sites

Discover Illinois: Kid's Zone

> Go to *http://www.teachercreated.com/books/3051*
> Click on page 79, site 1

National Geographic: Remembering Pearl Harbor

> Go to *http://www.teachercreated.com/books/3051*
> Click on page 79, site 2

Antarctica: A Virtual Tour

> Go to *http://www.teachercreated.com/books/3051*
> Click on page 79, site 3

Children of the Camps

> Go to *http://www.teachercreated.com/books/3051*
> Click on page 79, site 4

The History of the Holidays

> Go to *http://www.teachercreated.com/books/3051*
> Click on page 79, site 5

Iowa: Official State Web Site

> Go to *http://www.teachercreated.com/books/3051*
> Click on page 79, site 6

Official Web Site of Little Critter

> Go to *http://www.teachercreated.com/books/3051*
> Click on page 79, site 7

TSUM: Rosa Parks Library and Museum

> Go to *http://www.teachercreated.com/books/3051*
> Click on page 79, site 8

The Official Kwanzaa Site

> Go to *http://www.teachercreated.com/books/3051*
> Click on page 79, site 9

Key Words

- Antarctica
- Boston Tea Party
- Charles Dickens
- Christmas
- Dewey Decimal System
- Emporer Hirohito
- Hanukkah
- Holidays
- Illinois
- Indianapolis 500
- Iowa
- Kwanzaa
- Mercer Mayer
- Pearl Harbor
- Roald Amundsen
- Roller Skates
- Rosa Parks
- Scrooge
- Sitting Bull
- South Carolina
- St. Nicholas
- State of Illinois
- State of Iowa
- Tasmania
- Tasmanian Devil
- Thirteenth Amendment
- Times Square
- Transatlantic Radio
- Walt Disney
- Wassily Kandinsky

Calendar Grids

JANUARY

Sun	Mon	Tue	Wed	Thu	Fri	Sat

FEBRUARY

Sun	Mon	Tue	Wed	Thu	Fri	Sat

Calendar Grids *(cont.)*

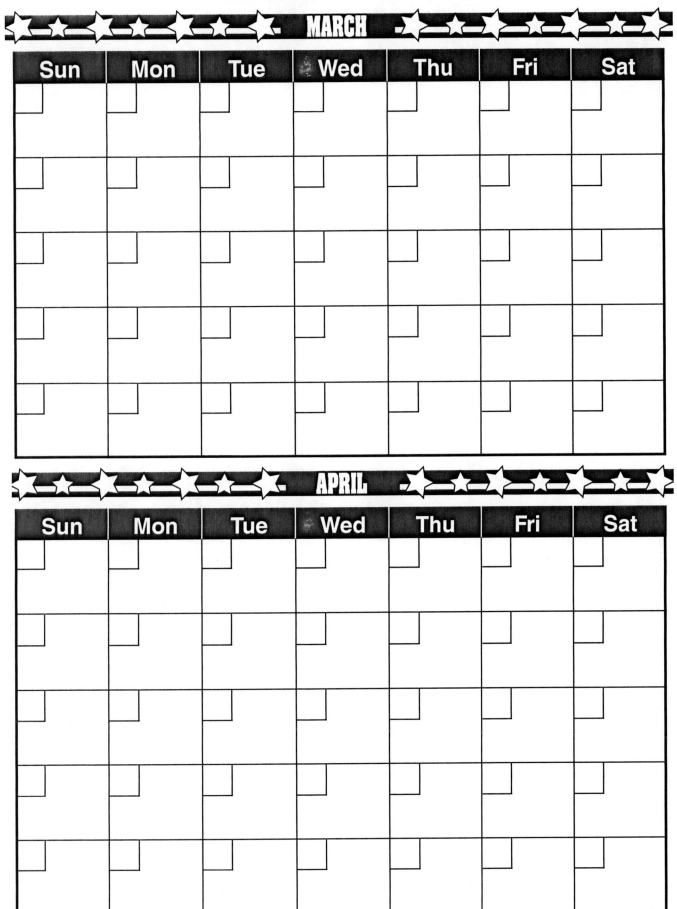

MARCH

Sun	Mon	Tue	Wed	Thu	Fri	Sat

APRIL

Sun	Mon	Tue	Wed	Thu	Fri	Sat

Calendar Grids *(cont.)*

MAY

Sun	Mon	Tue	Wed	Thu	Fri	Sat

JUNE

Sun	Mon	Tue	Wed	Thu	Fri	Sat

Calendar Grids *(cont.)*

JULY

Sun	Mon	Tue	Wed	Thu	Fri	Sat

AUGUST

Sun	Mon	Tue	Wed	Thu	Fri	Sat

Calendar Grids *(cont.)*

★ SEPTEMBER ★

Sun	Mon	Tue	Wed	Thu	Fri	Sat

★ OCTOBER ★

Sun	Mon	Tue	Wed	Thu	Fri	Sat

Calendar Grids *(cont.)*

★ ★ ★ ★ ★ ★ — NOVEMBER — ★ ★ ★ ★ ★ ★

Sun	Mon	Tue	Wed	Thu	Fri	Sat

★ ★ ★ ★ ★ ★ — DECEMBER — ★ ★ ★ ★ ★ ★

Sun	Mon	Tue	Wed	Thu	Fri	Sat

Note: Answers given to questions in italics are for information only.

January Answer Key

January 1

On January 1, 1863, President Abraham Lincoln issued a document called the Emancipation Proclamation. This document called for all slaves to be free. Many freed slaves chose to fight for the Union army.

January 2

On January 2, 1893, the U.S. Post Office issued the first commemorative postage stamp. It was made in honor of the four-hundredth anniversary of the discovery of America. Do you know anyone that collects stamps?

January 3

Alaska became the 49th state on January 3, 1959. Alaska is known for its rich natural resources like oil, gold, and trees. Alaska is our biggest state, and it also has a longer coastline than any other state.

January 4

Louis Braille was born on January 4, 1809. When he was three, he became blind because of an accident in his father's shop. He later invented the printing and writing system for the blind. A sign on the door of his house reads, "He opened the doors of knowledge to all those who cannot see."

January 5

George Washington Carver died on January 5, 1943. He was born in Missouri as a slave, but he later became a famous scientist. He experimented with peanuts and found over 300 different ways to use them, including to make soap, plastic, and paint.

January 6

Carl Sandburg was born on January 6, 1878. He was a famous poet, and he wrote many poems for children. Sandburg said, "If poems could be explained, then poets would have to leave out roses, sunsets, and faces from their poems."

January 7

The first presidential election in America took place on January 7, 1789. The person who won that election was a general in the army and helped the United States gain its independence from Great Britain. Do you know who was elected?
(Answer: *George Washington*)

Note: Answers given to questions in italics are for information only.

January Answer Key *(cont.)*

January 8

On January 8, 1815, the Battle of New Orleans was fought in the War of 1812. The battle was fought two weeks after the war was over. Why do you think the soldiers didn't know the war was over? (Answer: *The communication systems in those days were slow. They did not have telephones.*)

January 9

Richard Nixon was born on January 9, 1913. He was known for being very good at working with foreign leaders, but he is probably best remembered for being the only president who has ever resigned from office.

January 10

On January 10, 1946, people called "delegates" met for the first session of the United Nations General Assembly. They met after World War II ended to try to prevent such a terrible war from happening again.

January 11

On January 11, 1964, the U.S. Surgeon General's report declared cigarette smoking dangerous for your health. Smoking is dangerous because it can cause cancer, emphysema, and other lung problems.

January 12

Fairy tales have been around for hundreds of years, but Charles Perrault was the first to write down the tales of <u>Sleeping Beauty</u>, <u>Little Red Riding Hood</u>, <u>Cinderella,</u> and <u>Puss in Boots</u>. Charles Perrault was born on January 12, 1628.

January 13

Michael Bond, author of the Paddington Bear books, was born on January 13, 1926. He came up with the idea for Paddington when he saw a lonely teddy bear in a store on Christmas Eve and bought it for his wife. They named the bear "Paddington" because they lived near Paddington Station.

January 14

The Revolutionary War ended on January 14, 1784. This was the war in which America fought to gain its independence from Great Britain. After this war, America became known as the United States.

Note: Answers given to questions in italics are for information only.

January Answer Key *(cont.)*

January 15

Martin Luther King, Jr., was born on January 15, 1929. He encouraged people to use non-violence to gain equal rights for African Americans. In his most famous speech, he said, "I have a dream."

January 16

The U.S. National Aeronautics and Space Administration (NASA) accepted its first women candidates for astronauts on January 16, 1978. Sally Ride became the first woman in space in June 1983 aboard the <u>Challenger</u> Space Shuttle.

January 17

Benjamin Franklin was born on January 17, 1706. He was one of the first people to experiment with electricity. He invented the lightning rod, the Franklin stove, and bifocal glasses. He also helped write the Declaration of Independence.

Muhammad Ali was born on January 17, 1942. He was a professional boxer who became the heavyweight champion of the world. Ali always said, "I'm the greatest." He changed his name from Cassius Clay to Muhammad Ali when he became a Muslim.

January 18

On January 18, 1778, explorer James Cook discovered and named the Sandwich Islands. They were later named the Hawaiian Islands. Hawaii became our 50th state in 1959.

January 19

Robert E. Lee was born on January 19, 1807. He commanded the Confederate Army of the South during the Civil War. In this war, several southern states left the United States because they wanted to own slaves. Lee did not believe in slavery, but he was loyal to the South.

Note: Answers given to questions in italics are for information only.

January Answer Key *(cont.)*

January 20

Every four years a president is inaugurated on January 20. On January 20, 1961, John F. Kennedy made his inaugural speech. He said, "And so, my fellow Americans, ask not what your country can do for you; ask what you can do for your country."

January 21

The Pittsburgh Steelers became the first football team to win three Super Bowls on January 21, 1979. Do you know what other teams have also won three or more Super Bowls? (Answer: *Green Bay Packers, San Francisco 49ers, Washington Redskins, Dallas Cowboys*)

January 22

On January 22, 1905, the Russian Revolution began when Russian troops fired on marchers at the Winter Palace in St. Petersburg. The marchers were protesting unfair treatment by Czar Nicholas II. A czar is similar to a king.

January 23

John Hancock was born on January 23, 1737. He was the first person to sign the Declaration of Independence. He signed it in large bold letters and said, "There! King George can read that without his spectacles."

January 24

John Sutter found gold near his mill in Sacramento, California, on January 24, 1848. His discovery caused thousands of people to come to the area near San Francisco. This event is now known as the Gold Rush of 1848.

January 25

On January 25, 1924, the first Winter Olympics opened in Chamonix, France. For a long time the Winter and Summer Olympics were held in the same year. It was not until 1994 that the Winter and Summer Olympics were held in different years. Some of the sports in the Winter Olympics are skiing, ice skating, and hockey.

Note: Answers given to questions in italics are for information only.

January Answer Key *(cont.)*

January 26

Australia was first settled by colonists on January 26, 1788. Australia is the only country in the world that is also a continent. It is best known for its coral reef, kangaroos, and eucalyptus trees.

January 27

Wolfgang Amadeus Mozart was born on January 27, 1756. When Mozart was six, he could play the violin and organ and compose his own music. During his lifetime, Mozart wrote more than 600 pieces of music, but he died a very poor man when he was 35.

January 28

On January 28, 1986, one of the worst accidents in space history occurred. The Challenger 2 Space Shuttle exploded just after liftoff, and all seven astronauts inside died. Christa McAuliffe, the first teacher to go into space, was on board this flight.

January 29

William McKinley was born on January 29, 1843. He was the twenty-fifth president of the United States. Before he became president, he was a lawyer, a congressman, and the governor of Ohio. He was assassinated in Buffalo, New York, on September 6, 1901.

January 30

Franklin D. Roosevelt was born on January 30, 1882. He was elected president four times. He served in a wheelchair because he had polio as a child. Roosevelt helped the country get back on its feet after the Great Depression and was president during World War II.

January 31

Franz Peter Schubert was born on January 31, 1797. He was a great musical composer, and he wrote over 600 songs during his short life. Sometimes he wrote as many as eight songs in one day. He died when he was 31.

Note: Answers given to questions in italics are for information only.

February Answer Key

February 1

Langston Hughes was born on February 1, 1902. He was a very famous African-American poet. His most famous poem is called "Dreams," and he often wrote about the African-American experience.

February 2

February 2 is Groundhog Day. Every year in Punxsutawney, Pennsylvania, a groundhog named Phil comes out of his hole. If he sees his shadow, there will be six more weeks of winter.

February 3

Elizabeth Blackwell was born on February 3, 1821. She was the first American woman doctor. She earned her medical degree in Geneva, New York, in 1849. She later started the Women's Medical College to encourage other women to become doctors.

February 4

On February 4, 1902, Charles Lindbergh was born in Detroit, Michigan. He is most famous for making the first nonstop solo flight across the Atlantic Ocean. He flew from New York to Paris, France.

February 5

Alan Shepard became the fifth person to walk on the moon on February 5, 1971. Shepard and Edgar Mitchell stayed on the moon for 34 hours and even hit several golf balls off the moon with Shepard's golf club.

February 6

Babe Ruth was born on February 6, 1895. He became famous around the world when he played baseball for the New York Yankees. He held the record for 714 home runs until hank Aaron hit 715 in 1974.

Note: Answers given to questions in italics are for information only.

February Answer Key *(cont.)*

February 7

Laura Ingalls Wilder was born on February 7, 1867. She wrote the popular Little House books. She didn't begin writing the books until she was 65 years old. The books are based on her own life as she grew up on the American frontier.

February 8

Jules Verne was born on February 8, 1823. He wrote fantasy and science fiction books. Some of his books include Around the World in Eighty Days, 20,000 Leagues Under the Sea, and Journey to the Center of the Earth.

February 9

William Henry Harrison was our ninth president. He was born on February 9, 1773, and died only 32 days after becoming the president. That is the shortest amount of time that anyone has ever been president of the United States.

February 10

Mark Spitz was born on February 10, 1950. He began swimming in the Pacific Ocean off Honolulu, Hawaii, when he was two years old. Spitz set a world record at the 1972 Olympic games in Munich, Germany, when he won seven gold medals.

February 11

Thomas Alva Edison was born on February 11, 1847. He invented the light bulb, record player, and copying machine. He only had three months of formal education but invented 1100 things. He always said, "The brain that isn't used, rusts."

February 12

Abraham Lincoln was born on February 12, 1809. He is most famous for issuing the Emancipation Proclamation, which freed the slaves. He gave a very famous speech called the "Gettysburg Address." It begins, "Four score and seven years ago . . ."

Note: Answers given to questions in italics are for information only.

February Answer Key *(cont.)*

February 13

On February 13, 1635, the oldest public school in the United States was founded. It was named the Boston Public Latin School. In what state is the city of Boston?
(Answer: *Massachusetts*)

February 14

February 14 is Valentine's Day. This holiday is celebrated in honor of a man named Valentine who was a priest in Rome, Italy, when Christianity was a new religion. He was put to death for teaching Christianity but was later chosen to be a saint.

February 15

On February 15, 1564, Galileo Galilei was born. He believed that the earth revolved around the sun even though most people didn't agree. Today we know he was right. He also discovered four of Jupiter's moons using a telescope he designed himself.

February 16

On February 16, 1923, King Tut's tomb was opened by archaeologists. The tomb had been sealed for more than 3,000 years. Scientists have studied a lot about the way Egyptians mummified dead people to preserve the bodies.

February 17

Marian Anderson was born on February 17, 1902. She was a very famous singer, and she was the first black woman to perform with the Metropolitan Opera Company in New York. She said, "I have a great belief in the future of my people and my country."

February 18

Clyde Tombaugh, an astronomer, discovered Pluto on February 18, 1930. Pluto is the outermost planet of the nine planets in our solar system. It takes 248 years for Pluto to go around the sun, and it can only be seen with powerful telescopes.

Note: Answers given to questions in italics are for information only.

February Answer Key *(cont.)*

February 19

On February 19, 1878, inventor Thomas Edison patented the phonograph. These machines played music by turning a crank, and the sound came out of a large megaphone. Edison is most famous for inventing the light bulb.

February 20

Frederick Douglass died on February 20, 1895. He was born a slave, but he escaped and later bought his own freedom. He became an important journalist, statesman, and abolitionist. He worked with President Lincoln to end slavery.

February 21

The Washington Monument was dedicated on February 21, 1885. It was built in honor of George Washington. It is 555 feet high and is the tallest building in Washington, D.C.

February 22

George Washington was born on February 22, 1732. He was the first president of the United States and was the commander of the American Army during the Revolutionary War against Britain. He is known as the father of our country.

February 23

On February 23, 1836, the attack on the Alamo began in San Antonio, Texas. This battle was fought while Texas was trying to gain its independence from Mexico. The Texans lost but later gained their independence.

February 24

Wilhelm Grimm was born on February 24, 1786. He wrote German folktales and fairy tales. He wrote <u>Hansel and Gretel</u>, <u>The Ugly Duckling</u>, and <u>Snow White</u>.

Note: Answers given to questions in italics are for information only.

February Answer Key *(cont.)*

February 25

Pierre Auguste Renoir was born on February 25, 1841. He was an impressionist painter who lived in France. He began his career painting china in a factory but later became a very famous painter.

February 26

William Frederick Cody, better known as "Buffalo Bill," was born on February 26, 1864. He was born in Iowa and became a Pony Express rider and Army scout. He later organized a Wild West show and toured the United States and Europe.

February 27

Henry Wadsworth Longfellow was born on February 27, 1807. He was a poet. His most famous poem is "Paul Revere's Ride." The first line of the poem is, "Listen my children, and you shall hear of the midnight ride of Paul Revere."

February 28

The first shipload of gold-seekers arrived in San Francisco, California, on February 28, 1849. Gold is formed deep within the Earth's crust. It starts in liquid form because of the high temperatures and then becomes solid as it rises to the surface.

February 29

February 29 is Leap Year Day. The Roman Emperor, Julius Caesar, introduced a calendar for which his astronomers calculated the year to be 365 days and six hours long. In order to make up for the extra six hours, they added a day every fourth year.

(Note: There was still an error, so now leap years occur every fourth year except in century years not divisible by 400. For example, 1700 and 1900 were not leap years, but 2000 was.)

Note: Answers given to questions in italics are for information only.

March Answer Key

March 1

On March 1, 1867, Nebraska became the thirty-seventh state. The state flower is the goldenrod, the state tree is the cottonwood, and the state bird is the western meadowlark.

March 2

Theodore Seuss Geisel, better known as Dr. Seuss, was born on March 2, 1904. His first book, And to Think I Saw It on Mulberry Street, was rejected by 28 publishers before it was finally accepted. What is your favorite Dr. Seuss book?

March 3

Alexander Graham Bell was born on March 3, 1847. He worked with people who were hearing- and speech-impaired. During his research, he discovered a way to send sound through vibrations. This led him to invent the telephone.

March 4

Knute Rockne was born on March 4, 1888. He was the football coach at the University of Notre Dame and was one of the most successful coaches in football history. He was known for his motivating speeches and always said, "Win one for the Gipper."

March 5

The Boston Massacre occurred on March 5, 1770. A crowd of American colonists were throwing snowballs at British soldiers, and the soldiers fired, killing five colonists. A monument now marks this spot.

March 6

Michelangelo was born on March 6, 1475, in Italy. He was a sculptor, a painter, an architect, and a poet. His most famous sculptures are the Pieta and David. His most famous painting is on the ceiling of the Sistine Chapel.

March 7

Charles B. Darrow invented the game of Monopoly on March 7, 1933. When he first showed it to Parker Brothers, they were not interested. However, one year later, they decided to market it. The longest Monopoly game in history lasted 70 straight days.

Note: Answers given to questions in italics are for information only.

March Answer Key *(cont.)*

March 8

March 8 is International Women's Day. This holiday was first celebrated in 1909, and it is a national holiday in many countries. It is a day to honor women and remember their important contributions to the world.

March 9

Amerigo Vespucci was born on March 9, 1454. He was an Italian mapmaker who sailed west looking for a route to Asia, but he discovered Central and South America instead. The continents of North and South America are named after him.

March 10

On March 10, 1913, Harriet Tubman died in Auburn, New York. She was a slave who faced many dangers to lead slaves to freedom. Tubman said, "On my Underground Railroad, I never run my train off the track, and I never lost a passenger."

March 11

On March 11, 1888, the great blizzard struck the northeastern United States. This storm left 50 inches of snow in some states. About how many feet is 50 inches of snow? (Answer: *It is about four feet.*)

March 12

On March 12, 1912, Juliette Gordon Low founded the American Girl Scouts. She formed the first troop in Savannah, Georgia, and then traveled around the United States setting up different troops in all the states.

March 13

Astronomer William Herschel discovered Uranus on March 13, 1781. It is the seventh planet from the sun, and it has at least 11 thin rings around it. The rings are much fainter than those around Saturn.

Note: Answers given to questions in italics are for information only.

March Answer Key *(cont.)*

March 14

Albert Einstein was born on March 14, 1879, in Ulm, Germany. He was Jewish and came to the United States in 1933 to escape the Nazis. His research led to the development of television and the atom bomb.

March 15

March 15 is known as the Ides of March. Julius Caesar was assassinated at a meeting of the Roman Senate on March 15, 44 B.C. He was the leader of the Roman Empire over 2,000 years ago.

March 16

On March 16, 1926, Dr. Robert H. Goddard launched the first liquid propellant rocket outside Auburn, Massachusetts. It traveled 56 meters, and the flight lasted 2.5 seconds. His ideas helped to make airplanes and rockets possible.

March 17

March 17 is Saint Patrick's Day. Saint Patrick was born in England and was later captured and taken to Ireland as a slave. He escaped and became a missionary. He tried to convert the Irish to Christianity. Saint Patrick's Day marks the day of his death in A.D. 461.

March 18

President Grover Cleveland was born on March 18, 1837. He was the only president to lose a reelection and run again four years later and win. He got married while he was in office. He developed cancer of the mouth and had to wear a handmade jaw.

March 19

On March 19, 1975, Pennsylvania became the first state to allow girls to compete against boys in high school sports. Why do you think the state allowed girls to compete against boys?

Note: Answers given to questions in italics are for information only.

March Answer Key *(cont.)*

March 20

March 20, 1854, is recognized as the first meeting of the Republican Party. This party was founded to oppose the spread of slavery into western territories. The first Republican candidate to become president was Abraham Lincoln in 1860.

March 21

Benito Juarez was born on March 21, 1806. He is known as the George Washington of Mexico because he helped to gain Mexico's independence. He had to fight against the Spanish, the French, and the Austrians in order to free his country.

March 22

Randolph Caldecott was born on March 22, 1846. He was born in Chester, England, and began drawing when he was a young boy. The Caldecott Medal is awarded each year to the illustrator of the most distinguished picture book.

March 23

On March 23, 1775, Patrick Henry gave a very famous speech. In the speech, he said, "Give me liberty, or give me death." Henry was a leader during the Revolutionary War and encouraged the colonists to fight for independence from Great Britain.

March 24

On March 24, 1989, the Exxon Valdez ran aground in Prince William Sound off the coast of Alaska. The ship spilled almost 11 million gallons of oil. Many birds, animals, and fish were killed because they were covered in oil or ate fish covered in oil.

March 25

Gutzon Borglum was born on March 25, 1871. He is an American sculptor who is best known for carving Mount Rushmore in South Dakota. The memorial contains the heads of George Washington, Thomas Jefferson, Abraham Lincoln, and Theodore Roosevelt.

Note: Answers given to questions in italics are for information only.

March Answer Key *(cont.)*

March 26

Robert Frost was born on March 26, 1874. He was a famous poet who wrote "Stopping by Woods on a Snowy Evening." Robert did not attend school until he was 12 years old and never read a book until he was 14. He said, "Every poem solves something for me in life."

March 27

The strongest earthquake in American history shook Alaska on March 27, 1964. It measured 9.2 on the Richter scale and created a huge tsunami, or tidal wave, that killed 115 people.

March 28

President George Bush awarded the Congressional Gold Medal to Jesse Owens on March 28, 1990. Owens won four gold medals in track-and-field events in the 1936 Olympics, which were held in Berlin, Germany.

March 29

The first permanent white settlement in North America was established on March 29, 1638. Under the leadership of a man named Peter Minuit, Swedish settlers founded it. The settlement was in what is now the state of Delaware.

March 30

Vincent Van Gogh was born on March 30, 1853. During his lifetime, he only sold one of his paintings, but they are worth millions today. He said, "There is nothing in the world as interesting as people. One can never study them enough."

March 31

The Eiffel Tower was completed on March 31, 1889. It was built by Alexandre Gustave Eiffel and was the tallest building in the world at the time. It is 985 feet high. Eiffel built the tower for the World's Fair in Paris.

Note: *Answers given to questions in italics are for information only.*

April Answer Key

April 1

April 1 is called April Fool's Day. It was first celebrated in France because the first day of spring and the New Year both fell on April 1. Even after the New Year was changed, some people still celebrated it, and they were called "fools."

April 2

Hans Christian Anderson was born on April 2, 1805. He was a poet, an author, and a playwright, but he is best known for his fairy tales. He wrote "The Ugly Duckling," "The Emperor's New Clothes," and "The Snow Queen."

April 3

Jane Goodall was born on April 3, 1934. She is an expert on chimpanzees and has studied chimps in Africa for over 30 years. She is worried about the survival of chimps, and she is trying to find other solutions to live animal research.

April 4

Martin Luther King, Jr., was shot and killed on April 4, 1968, in Memphis, Tennessee. King believed in non-violence, but riots broke out in many big cities after his death.

April 5

Booker T. Washington was born on April 5, 1856, as a slave in Virginia. After becoming free, he went to school and later started the Tuskegee Institute. He hoped blacks could gain equality through education.

April 6

Matthew Henson, an African-American explorer, discovered the North Pole on April 6, 1909. Henson made two earlier trips but had failed to reach the North Pole. Finally, on his third try, he succeeded. Robert Peary and four Eskimos accompanied him on this historic expedition.

On April 6, 1896, the first modern Olympic games were held in Athens, Greece. People from thirteen countries came to the events. Some of the events included foot races, discus throwing, jumping, and wrestling.

Note: Answers given to questions in italics are for information only.

April Answer Key *(cont.)*

April 7

April 7 is World Health Day. Everyone is encouraged to eat healthy, get enough sleep, and exercise. However, in poorer countries, doctors make sure that people have enough to eat and proper medical care.

April 8

On April 8, 1974, Hank Aaron hit his 715th home run for the Atlanta Braves. This home run broke Babe Ruth's record of 714 home runs. Aaron finished his career with 775 home runs.

April 9

On April 9, 1833, the first free public library opened in Peterborough, New Hampshire. Some of the taxes people pay are used for libraries. A man named Andrew Carnegie donated 50 million dollars to build libraries in our country.

April 10

The U.S. patent system was established on April 10, 1790. Some things that have been patented are the zipper, the safety pin, the toothpick, and the eraser-tipped pencil.

April 11

Iowa became the first state to impose a cigarette tax on April 11, 1921. This meant that people had to pay extra for their cigarettes. There is also a tax on alcohol. Why do you think the government taxes these kinds of items?

On April 11, 1968, one week after the assassination of Martin Luther King, Jr., President Lyndon Johnson signed the Civil Rights Act of 1968 into law. One of the reasons for passing the law was to protect civil rights workers from violence.

Note: Answers given to questions in italics are for information only.

April Answer Key *(cont.)*

April 12

On April 12, 1961, Yuri Gagarin became the first man in space. He was from the Soviet Union, and he made one orbit around the earth aboard the spacecraft <u>Vostok I</u>.

April 13

Thomas Jefferson was born on April 13, 1743. He was one of the authors of the Declaration of Independence, and he was the third president. He purchased the Louisiana Territory and helped plan the city of Washington, D.C.

April 14

President Abraham Lincoln was assassinated on April 14, 1865 by a man named John Wilkes Booth. After Booth shot Lincoln at the Ford's Theatre, he jumped to the stage and broke one of his legs. Lincoln died the next day in a house near the theater.

April 15

Leonardo da Vinci was born on April 15, 1452. He was a great painter, sculptor, and inventor. He is most famous for his painting of the <u>Mona Lisa</u> in Paris, France.

The <u>Titanic</u> sank on April 15, 1912, after hitting an iceberg in the Atlantic Ocean. More than 1,500 people were killed because the ship hadn't carried enough lifeboats. In 1985, the ship was discovered on the ocean floor, sitting 2.5 miles below the water's surface.

April 16

On April 16, 1503, Christopher Columbus left Veragua in Central America to begin his trip back to Europe. This was his last voyage to America.

Note: *Answers given to questions in italics are for information only.*

April Answer Key *(cont.)*

April 17

The <u>Apollo 13</u> spacecraft landed safely in the Pacific Ocean on April 17, 1970. During the mission, one of the oxygen tanks exploded, and the astronauts were not sure they had enough energy to return to Earth. One of the astronauts said, "Houston, we have a problem."

April 18

On April 18, 1775, Paul Revere began his famous ride to warn the American colonists that the British were coming. He left Boston, Massachusetts, at 10 P.M. and arrived in Lexington at midnight to warn Sam Adams and John Hancock.

April 19

The Battle of Lexington and Concord took place on April 19, 1775. This was the first battle of the American Revolution. Why were Americans fighting the British? (Answer: *to gain their independence from Great Britain*)

April 20

Adolf Hitler was born on April 20, 1889. He is known for being the leader of Germany and the Nazi party. When he took over several countries in Europe, World War II began. He is responsible for the death of over six million Jews in Europe.

April 21

A German educator named Friedrich Froebel was born on April 21, 1882. He started the first kindergarten in 1837. The word kindergarten means "children's garden." The idea of kindergarten has since spread throughout the world.

April 22

The first Earth Day was celebrated on April 22, 1970. Twenty million Americans participated in marches and rallies to protest pollution. Twenty years later, on April 22, 1990, 200 million people participated in Earth Day in 141 different countries.

April 23

William Shakespeare was born on April 23, 1564. He was a great English poet and playwright. He wrote <u>Romeo and Juliet</u>, <u>Hamlet</u>, and <u>Macbeth</u>.

Note: Answers given to questions in italics are for information only.

April Answer Key *(cont.)*

April 24

The first American League baseball game was played between Cleveland and Chicago on April 24, 1901. Chicago won by a score of 8 to 2. In what two states are these cities? (Answer: *Cleveland is in Ohio; Chicago is in Illinois.*)

April 25

On April 25, 1901, New York became the first state to require automobile license plates. It cost $1.00 to buy the plates. Why do states require drivers to put license plates on their cars? (Answer: *License plates allow cars to be easily identified by law enforcement officials.*)

April 26

Charles Richter was born on April 26, 1900. He was a seismologist who developed the Richter Scale. This scale measures the force of earthquakes. A quake of less than 3.0 is hardly noticeable, but a quake of 6.0 can cause buildings to shake.

April 27

Ulysses S. Grant was born on April 27, 1822. He was the eighteenth president of the United States. He was also the commander of the Union Army during the Civil War. The Transcontinental Railroad was finished during his presidency.

April 28

James Monroe was born on April 28, 1758. He was the fifth U.S. president and the only other president besides George Washington to run unopposed. What does "unopposed" mean? (Answer: *"Unopposed" means that no one ran against the candidate. In this case it was Monroe.*)

April 29

On April 29, 1913, Gideon Sundback patented the zipper. He called it a "separable fastener," because you could separate the two parts from each other and then fasten them back together again.

April 30

On April 30, 1803, Napoleon sold the Louisiana Territory to President Thomas Jefferson for about two cents per acre. It was the largest land purchase in world history. What states were included in the Louisiana Territory? (Answer: *All of Louisiana, Arkansas, Missouri, Nebraska, South Dakota, North Dakota, and Iowa were in the territory. Parts of Montana, Colorado, Wyoming, Oklahoma, Mississippi, Alabama, Kansas, and Minnesota were also in the territory.*)

Note: *Answers given to questions in italics are for information only.*

May Answer Key

May 1

The Empire State Building was opened to the public on May 1, 1931. It has 102 stories and is one of the tallest buildings in the world. The Sears Tower in Chicago is now the tallest building in the United States.

May 2

Alaska's flag was adopted on May 2, 1927. A seventh-grade student designed the flag. Alaska didn't become a state until 1959. Where could you find a picture of Alaska's flag? (Answer: *atlas, encyclopedia, other reference book, Internet*)

May 3

Golda Meir was born on May 3, 1898. She was born in Russia but later moved to Milwaukee, Wisconsin. After she got married, she moved to Palestine and worked for the government. She eventually became the prime minister of Israel.

May 4

On May 4, 1626, Peter Minuit landed on Manhattan Island and eventually bought it for $24.00 from the Native Americans who were living there. He paid for it with beads and trinkets.

May 5

Nellie Bly was born on May 5, 1867. She was the first female journalist to achieve world-wide fame. She wrote many stories about her courageous adventures, and she traveled around the world in less than 80 days.

May 6

The Hindenburg, a giant balloon-like vehicle, exploded as it prepared to land in Lakehurst, New Jersey, on May 6, 1937. It had just finished a flight across the Atlantic Ocean. It was filled with a very explosive gas called hydrogen.

May 7

Peter Tchaikovsky was born on May 7, 1840. He composed music and produced symphonies, operas, and ballets. His ballets include Swan Lake, Sleeping Beauty, and The Nutcracker.

Note: *Answers given to questions in italics are for information only.*

May Answer Key *(cont.)*

May 8

Harry S. Truman was born on May 8, 1884. He became our twenty-third president. As president, he forced the end of World War II by ordering the U.S. military to drop atomic bombs on the Japanese cities of Hiroshima and Nagasaki.

May 9

Howard Carter was born on May 9, 1873. He discovered King Tut's tomb in Egypt in 1922. King Tut's tomb consisted of three rooms with couches, food, jewelry, and boats inside.

May 10

On May 10, 1869, the first transcontinental railroad was completed near Promontory, Utah. A golden spike was used to connect Omaha, Nebraska, to Sacramento, California.

May 11

Minnesota became the thirty-second state on May 11, 1858. Its state flower is the pink and white lady's slipper, and the state bird is the common loon.

May 12

Florence Nightingale was born on May 12, 1820, in Florence, Italy. She nursed injured soldiers during wars, and she is considered the founder of modern nursing.

May 13

On May 13, 1607, Captain John Smith and 105 colonists founded the Jamestown colony in Virginia. This was the first permanent English settlement in America.

Note: Answers given to questions in italics are for information only.

May Answer Key *(cont.)*

May 14

Gabriel Daniel Fahrenheit was born on May 14, 1686. In 1714, he invented the type of thermometer that is used today. The Fahrenheit temperature scale is named after him. Some thermometers have a metric temperature scale, which is named after someone else. What is the name of the metric temperature scale? (Answer: *the Celcius scale*)

May 15

L. Frank Baum was born on May 15, 1856. He wrote the book The Wizard of Oz, and his story was later made into a movie. He also wrote 13 other books about Oz because people liked his first book so much.

May 16

William Seward was born on May 16, 1801. He was the Secretary of State and arranged for the purchase of Alaska. He ran against Abraham Lincoln for the Republican nomination for president but lost. He was also shot the same night as President Lincoln, but he survived.

May 17

On May 17, 1954, there was a very important Supreme Court decision. It was called Brown vs. Board of Education of Topeka, Kansas, and it said that separating blacks and whites in different schools was unfair and against the law.

May 18

On May 18, 1980, Mt. St. Helens erupted in the state of Washington. It is considered the worst volcanic disaster in the recorded history of the United States.

May 19

Malcolm X was born on May 19, 1925. He led a black religious movement called the Nation of Black Muslims. Many Muslims used the letter *X* as a last name rather than the names given to their ancestors by slave owners. Malcolm X was shot while giving a speech in New York.

Note: Answers given to questions in italics are for information only.

May Answer Key *(cont.)*

May 20

On May 20, 1932, Amelia Earhart began her famous flight across the Atlantic Ocean. She was the first woman to fly alone across the Atlantic. During a later flight, she crashed and neither she nor her plane has ever been found.

May 21

On May 21, 1927, Charles Lindbergh finished his first solo flight across the Atlantic Ocean. He flew from Long Island, New York, to Paris, France, in his plane called the Spirit of St. Louis. The flight took 33.5 hours.

May 22

Sir Arthur Conan Doyle was born on May 22, 1859. He was a British author, and he wrote mysteries about a character named Sherlock Holmes. *What is your favorite mystery?*

May 23

South Carolina became the eighth state on May 23, 1788. The state reptile is the loggerhead turtle. The loggerheads make nests along the eastern coast of South Carolina and are considered a threatened species.

May 24

On May 24, 1869, John Wesley Powell led the first expedition of the Grand Canyon. He and nine men traveled by boat from the Green River in Wyoming to the Colorado River, which has shaped the Grand Canyon.

May 25

On May 25, 1787, the Constitutional Convention opened in Philadelphia, Pennsylvania, with George Washington as president. Many men came to help write the Constitution, which stated the laws for the United States.

Note: Answers given to questions in italics are for information only.

May Answer Key *(cont.)*

May 26

Sally Ride was born on May 26, 1951. In June 1983, she was the first woman accepted into the astronaut program. She also became the first woman in space when she traveled on the space shuttle Challenger with four other astronauts.

May 27

The Golden Gate Bridge opened in San Francisco on May 27, 1937. It is one of the largest and most spectacular suspension bridges in the world. The bridge is 8,981 feet long and is named after the Golden Gate Strait at the entrance to San Francisco Bay.

May 28

Jim Thorpe was born on May 28, 1886. He is one of the greatest athletes in history. He was born in Prague, Oklahoma. Thorpe played major-league baseball, professional football, and ran track and field.

May 29

John F. Kennedy was born on May 29, 1917, in Brookline, Massachusetts. He was the 35th president, and he fought for equal rights for African Americans. He was assassinated in Dallas, Texas, on November 22, 1963.

May 30

Memorial Day was first officially observed on May 30, 1868. Graves of American soldiers are decorated with flowers on this day. This holiday was first begun to honor Civil War veterans and is now observed on the last Monday in May.

May 31

Walt Whitman, a famous American poet, was born on May 31, 1819. He wrote the poem "O Captain! My Captain!" as a tribute to Abraham Lincoln. He also cared for injured Union soldiers during the Civil War.

Note: Answers given to questions in italics are for information only.

June Answer Key

June 1

Happy Birthday, Kentucky and Tennessee! On June 1, 1792, Kentucky became the 15th state, and on June 1, 1796, Tennessee became the 16th state. Tennessee later seceded during the Civil War and was readmitted in 1866.

June 2

Martha Dandridge was born on June 2, 1731. After her first husband died, Martha married George Washington. Martha Washington was the first First Lady of the United States.

June 3

Charles Drew, an African-American surgeon, was born on June 3, 1904. He discovered a way to store blood for transfusions, which saved many lives during World War II. He quit his job to protest the separate storage of black and white people's blood.

June 4

On June 4, 1896, Henry Ford successfully test drove his first car on the streets of Detroit, Michigan. It was a horseless carriage called a Quadriycle.

June 5

Robert F. Kennedy was shot in a Los Angeles, California, hotel on June 5, 1968. He had just won the Democratic Presidential Primary in California. He died the next day.

June 6

British, Canadian, and American troops invaded the beaches of Normandy, France, on June 6, 1944. This invasion is known as D-Day and was very important because it lead to the end of World War II.

June 7

On June 7, 1776, Richard Henry Lee of Virginia proposed a Declaration of Independence to the Continental Congress. He said, "These United Colonies are, and of right ought to be, free and independent states."

Note: Answers given to questions in italics are for information only.

June Answer Key *(cont.)*

June 8

Frank Lloyd Wright was born on June 8, 1867. He was a famous architect who designed buildings that related in some way to their natural surroundings.

June 9

George Stephenson was born on June 9, 1781. He is considered the father of the railway system, and he built a fast locomotive called <u>Rocket</u> that could carry passengers. He didn't attend a formal school until he was 19.

June 10

On June 10, 1928, Maurice Sendak was born. He has written more than 80 children's books, but his most famous one is <u>Where the Wild Things Are</u>. He has won the Caldecott Medal and the American Book Award.

June 11

Jacques Cousteau was born in France on June 11, 1910. He spent much of his life exploring the oceans, and he helped invent the SCUBA gear, which allows divers to breathe underwater.

June 12

Anne Frank was born on June 12, 1929. She and her family hid from the Nazis in Holland during World War II. They were eventually found by the Germans, and Anne later died in a concentration camp. Her diary helped the world understand her family's story.

June 13

President Lyndon Johnson appointed Thurgood Marshall to the United States Supreme Court on June 13, 1967. He was the first African-American Supreme Court justice, and he served until 1991.

June 14

Today is Flag Day! On June 14, 1777, the Continental Congress adopted the national flag. They ruled that it should have thirteen red and white stripes and thirteen stars for the original thirteen colonies. How many stars does the flag have now?
(Answer: *50 stars*)

Note: *Answers given to questions in italics are for information only.*

June Answer Key *(cont.)*

June 15

On June 15, 1752, Benjamin Franklin flew a kite during a thunderstorm to prove that lightning carries an electric charge. It is, in part, due to him that we have electric lights, televisions, and computers.

June 16

Valentina Tereshkova became the first woman in space on June 16, 1963. She was from the Soviet Union and traveled around the Earth 45 times in three days. She parachuted back to Earth after her spacecraft, the Vostok 6, reentered Earth's atmosphere.

June 17

Five burglars were arrested breaking into the Democratic Party Headquarters in the Watergate Hotel on June 17, 1972. The crime and the attempt to cover it up were linked to President Richard Nixon. He later resigned from office.

June 18

The children's book author and illustrator Chris van Allsburg was born on June 18, 1949. He has won two Caldecott Medals and wrote the books The Polar Express, Jumanji, and Just a Dream.

June 19

It's Juneteenth! June 19 is a day on which many African Americans celebrate the end of slavery. On June 19, 1865, Union soldiers landed at Galveston, Texas. They announced that the Civil War was over and that all slaves were free.

June 20

On June 20, 1782, Congress approved the Great Seal of the United States. Charles Thomson redesigned the seal after the Continental Congress rejected the first design, which was made by Ben Franklin, John Adams, and Thomas Jefferson.

June 21

On June 21, 1788, New Hampshire became the ninth state in the United States. The Constitution was officially adopted after New Hampshire became the ninth state to ratify it.

Note: Answers given to questions in italics are for information only.

June Answer Key *(cont.)*

June 22

The 26th Amendment was signed on June 22, 1970. This amendment changed the legal voting age from 21 to 18. How many years will it be until you are old enough to vote?

June 23

Wilma Rudolph, an African-American athlete, was born on June 23, 1940. She had polio as a child and wore a steel brace for six years, but she worked hard to succeed in basketball and track. She was the first American to win three gold medals during one Olympic games.

June 24

Henry VIII was crowned King of England at the age of 18 on June 24, 1509. He was very well educated and loved music and poetry, but he was also extremely cruel and had two of his wives beheaded.

June 25

Eric Carle, an author and illustrator of children's books, was born on June 25, 1929. He wrote and illustrated <u>The Very Hungry Caterpillar</u>, <u>The Very Quiet Cricket</u>, and <u>The Very Grouchy Ladybug</u>.

June 26

One of the greatest female athletes in history was born on June 26, 1914. Her name was "Babe" Didrikson Zaharias. She competed in swimming, basketball, golf, and track and field.

June 27

On June 27, 1922, the first Newbery Medal was awarded to Henrik Van Loon for his book <u>The Story of Mankind</u>. The medal is awarded to the most distinguished children's book published each year.

June 28

On June 28, 1894, Congress made the first Monday in September a national holiday. The holiday was called Labor Day and was created to celebrate the contributions that workers make to our country.

Note: Answers given to questions in italics are for information only.

June Answer Key *(cont.)*

June 29

George Washington Goethals was born on June 29, 1858. He was the chief engineer of the Panama Canal, a passageway for ships that runs between North and South America. Before it was built, ships had to sail around the tip of South America.

June 30

David McPhail, an author and illustrator of children's books, was born on June 30, 1940. He often writes books about bears, and one of his first books was <u>The Bear's Toothache</u>. He has written or illustrated over 40 books. Wow!

JULY

July Answer Key

July 1

Diana Spencer, who later became the Princess of Wales, was born on July 1, 1961. She married Prince Charles in 1981, and they had two sons, William and Henry. Princess Diana was killed in a car accident in Paris on August 30, 1997.

July 2

On July 2, 1964, President Lyndon Johnson signed the Civil Rights Act of 1964. This law banned discrimination because of a person's skin color, religion, gender, or race.

July 3

The Battle of Gettysburg ended on July 3, 1863. It was fought in Pennsylvania during the Civil War, and it was a victory for the Union Army of the North. However, more than 45,000 lives were lost in the battle.

July 4

On July 4, 1776, the Continental Congress adopted the Declaration of Independence, which was written by Thomas Jefferson. This document declared our independence from England and was signed by 56 men.

July 5

Phineas Taylor Barnum was born on July 5, 1810. He started P.T. Barnum's Traveling Circus in 1870. He later asked James Bailey to be his partner, and they formed the Barnum and Bailey Circus.

Note: Answers given to questions in italics are for information only.

July Answer Key *(cont.)*

July 6

The first All-Star baseball game was played on July 6, 1933. Babe Ruth hit the first home run in that game. It was played at Comiskey Park in Chicago, Illinois.

July 7

On July 7, 1981, President Ronald Reagan announced that he was nominating Judge Sandra Day O'Connor to the United States Supreme Court. She was the first female to become a Supreme Court judge.

July 8

On July 8, 1776, the Liberty Bell was rung to gather people so they could hear the Declaration of Independence read out loud. There are many stories about how the bell cracked. You can see the Liberty Bell in Philadelphia, Pennsylvania.

July 9

Elias Howe was born on July 9, 1819. He was the inventor of the sewing machine. Tailors and seamstresses did not like the sewing machine because they thought they would be out of a job.

July 10

Mary McLeod Bethune was born on July 10, 1875. She started a school for African-American girls in Daytona, Florida, in 1904. The school later became Bethune-Cookman College. Mary also worked with four different presidents to improve the lives of her people.

July 11

On July 11, 1899, children's book author E.B. White was born. He lived on a farm in Maine and often wrote about the animals that lived there. Can you name his most famous book about a pig and a spider? (Answer: *Charlotte's Web*)

July 12

George Eastman, inventor of the Kodak camera, was born on July 12, 1854. He and William Walker invented film that could be rolled and advanced through a camera. Up until this time, photographers were using a separate plate for each picture taken.

Note: Answers given to questions in italics are for information only.

July Answer Key *(cont.)*

July 13

Father Edward Flanagan was born on July 13, 1886. He was born in Ireland and came to the United States to become a priest. He later started Boys Town, a caring home for troubled boys in Omaha, Nebraska. It is now called Girls and Boys Town.

July 14

Gerald Ford was born on July 14, 1913, in Omaha, Nebraska. He was the 38th president of the United States and took over after Richard Nixon resigned from office.

July 15

On July 15, 1606, Rembrandt was born in the Netherlands. He was a Dutch painter who was famous for his use of light and shadow. He painted many portraits and landscapes.

July 16

The first atomic bomb was tested in a desert in New Mexico on July 16, 1945. The explosion was equal to almost 20,000 tons of dynamite. It created a 1,200-foot crater in the ground.

July 17

Disneyland opened in Anaheim, California, on July 17, 1955. Walt Disney designed this amusement park. Disney theme parks have also opened in Florida, France, and Japan.

July 18

John Glenn was born on July 18, 1921. He was the first American to orbit the earth and one of the first astronauts in the space program. He also became the oldest man to fly in space in 1998 at the age of 77.

Note: Answers given to questions in italics are for information only.

July Answer Key *(cont.)*

July 19

The first women's rights convention was held in Seneca Falls, New York, on July 19, 1848. Elizabeth Cady Stanton and three other women met to demand equal rights for women, including the right to vote.

July 20

On July 20, 1969, Buzz Aldrin and Neil Armstrong became the first men to set foot on the moon. Armstrong said, "That's one small step for man, one giant step for mankind."

July 21

The Battle of Bull Run took place on July 21, 1861. It was the first major battle of the Civil War and was a victory for the South. General Jackson got the nickname "Stonewall" as a result of this battle.

July 22

Alexander Calder was born on July 22, 1898. He was a sculptor who used mainly wire and metal in his artwork. He is considered to be the inventor of the mobile.

July 23

Ford Motor Company sold its first car on July 23, 1903. The car was called a Model A. Henry Ford started the company in June of 1903.

July 24

On July 24, 1847, Brigham Young and his followers arrived in the Valley of the Great Salt Lake in Utah. They had traveled from Illinois and were seeking a safe place to practice the Mormon religion.

Note: Answers given to questions in italics are for information only.

July Answer Key *(cont.)*

July 25

On July 25, 1952, Puerto Rico became a self-governing commonwealth of the United States. This means that Puerto Ricans follow some of the laws of the United States, and they make some of their own laws too.

July 26

New York became the 11th state to join the United States on July 26, 1788. The state flower is the rose, and the state muffin is the apple muffin. What is the capital of New York? (Answer: *Albany*)

July 27

Bugs Bunny first appeared in a cartoon on July 27, 1940. The cartoon was entitled <u>A Wild Hare</u>. Chuck Jones created Bugs Bunny, Daffy Duck, Porky Pig, and many other cartoon characters.

July 28

Beatrix Potter, the author of children's books, was born on July 28, 1866. She grew up in London and had many pets. Most of the characters in her books are based on the pets she had as a child.

July 29

Charles William Beebe, an ocean explorer, was born on July 29, 1877. He and Otis Barton dove more than 3000 feet down into the ocean in a steel ball called a bathysphere. Beebe was interested in finding new creatures that had never been seen before.

July 30

On July 30, 1863, Henry Ford was born in Dearborn Township, Michigan. He started Ford Motor Company and came up with the idea to use an assembly line to make cars much faster. This was called mass production.

July 31

J.K. Rowling was born on July 31, 1965. She is the author of the Harry Potter series about a boy who attends the Hogwarts School of Witchcraft and Wizardry.

Note: *Answers given to questions in italics are for information only.*

August Answer Key

August 1

On August 1, 1770, the explorer William Clark was born. He and Meriweather Lewis led an expedition to explore the western United States. They drew maps of the land and kept journals of their travels to share with the American people.

August 2

Saddam Hussein, the leader of Iraq, ordered his army to invade Kuwait on August 2, 1990. President George Bush sent U.S. troops to Saudi Arabia to help Kuwait. This action was called Operation Desert Storm.

August 3

On August 3, 1610, English explorer Henry Hudson discovered a large bay on the east coast of Canada. He named it Hudson Bay. He and his crew were looking for a passage to the Pacific Ocean.

August 4

The U.S. Coast Guard was established on August 4, 1790. It was created to enforce customs laws because the country was having problems with smuggling. The Coast Guard is able to board and search any vessel in U.S. waters.

August 5

Neil Armstrong was born on August 5, 1930. He was the first person to walk on the moon. He was the commander of the <u>Apollo 11</u> mission. The other astronauts on board were Buzz Aldrin and Mike Collins.

August 6

On August 6, 1945, the United States dropped an atomic bomb on Hiroshima, Japan, in an effort to end World War II. The bomb killed nearly 140,000 people and was the first time a nuclear weapon had been used in war.

Note: Answers given to questions in italics are for information only.

August Answer Key *(cont.)*

August 7

On August 27, 1927, the International Peace Bridge opened between Buffalo, New York, and Fort Erie, Ontario. It was dedicated to 100 years of friendship between the U.S. and Canada, the longest standing friendship between two countries that share a border.

August 8

Matthew Henson was born on August 8, 1866. He was an African-American explorer who was the first person to reach the North Pole. The leader of the expedition, Robert Peary, arrived 45 minutes later.

August 9

The United States dropped a second atomic bomb on Japan on August 9, 1945. The bomb was dropped on the city of Nagasaki and killed an estimated 74,000 people.

August 10

On August 10, 1846, Congress chartered the Smithsonian Institution after James Smithson gave $500,000 to set it up. The Smithsonian Institution is made up of 16 museums and galleries and the national zoo.

August 11

Joanna Cole was born on August 11, 1944. She and Bruce Degen have written the many books in the Magic School Bus series. Cole said, "Writing is hard work, but it's the greatest fun in the world."

August 12

Katherine Lee Bates was born on August 12, 1859. She was the author and composer of the song "America the Beautiful." The first line is, "Oh, beautiful for spacious skies, for amber waves of grain."

Note: Answers given to questions in italics are for information only.

August Answer Key *(cont.)*

August 13

On August 13, 1926, Fidel Castro, the president of Cuba, was born. He has been the Communist leader of Cuba since 1959, when he and his army took over this island country off the coast of Florida.

August 14

Japan surrendered to the United States on August 14, 1945. After the bombing of Nagasaki and Hiroshima, Japanese Emperor Hirohito said, "We cannot continue the war any longer." This ended World War II and is often called V-J Day.

August 15

On August 15, 1769, Napoleon Bonaparte was born. He was the Emperor of France and the leader of the French revolution. He was defeated by the British at the Battle of Waterloo and forced to give up his empire.

August 16

Matt Christopher, a children's book author, was born on August 16, 1917. When Matt was a child, his favorite sport was baseball. As an adult, he wrote many books about sports.

August 17

Davy Crockett was born on August 17, 1786, in Tennessee. He was a congressman, a soldier, and a hunter. He died fighting in the Battle of the Alamo in 1836.

August 18

Roberto Clemente was born in Puerto Rico on August 18, 1934. He was a baseball player for the Pittsburgh Pirates. He died in a plane crash on December 31, 1972, and was the first Hispanic player to be inducted into the Baseball Hall of Fame.

Note: Answers given to questions in italics are for information only.

August Answer Key *(cont.)*

August 19

On August 19, 1871, Orville Wright was born. Orville and his brother Wilbur invented and built the first controlled airplane. Orville was the first to fly this plane, and he stayed in the air for 12 seconds.

August 20

Vitus Bering was chosen by Peter the Great to find a land connecting Asia and North America. There was no such land to be found, but, on August 20, 1741, he discovered Alaska. The Bering Strait and Bering Island are named after him.

August 21

Hawaii became the 50th state on August 21, 1959. It was the last state to be admitted to the United States. It is made up of eight main islands, and its capital is Honolulu.

August 22

On August 22, 1864, twelve nations signed the Geneva Convention, which established the Red Cross and made rules for how to treat wounded people and how to protect medical workers. Clara Barton established the American Red Cross in 1881.

August 23

On August 23, 1775, King George III of England refused the American colonists' offers of peace and declared that the colonists were in rebellion. The American Revolution had already begun.

August 24

Mount Vesuvius erupted on August 24 in A.D. 79. It destroyed the Roman cities of Pompeii and Herculaneum. Around 20,000 people were killed in the eruption.

August 25

On August 25, 1916, the National Park Service was created within the Department of the Interior. There are approximately 380 national parks in the United States. Some of these include the Grand Canyon, the Washington Monument, and the Everglades.

Note: *Answers given to questions in italics are for information only.*

August Answer Key *(cont.)*

August 26

The Nineteenth Amendment went into effect on August 26, 1920. This amendment guaranteed women the right to vote. It had first been introduced to Congress in 1878.

August 27

Mother Theresa was born on August 27, 1910. She was a nun who pledged her life to helping the poor. She was awarded the Nobel Peace Prize and the Medal of Freedom for her work. How old was Mother Theresa when she died on September 5, 1997? (Answer: *She was 87 years old.*)

August 28

On August 28, 1963, Martin Luther King, Jr., led the famous march on Washington, D.C. He gave a speech to over 200,000 people from the steps of the Lincoln Memorial. It was called "I Have a Dream."

August 29

Francisco Pizarro killed the Incan King Atahualpa on August 29, 1533. Pizarro and 200 Spanish conquistadors had destroyed the Incan civilization in search of gold in South America.

August 30

Donald Crews, the children's book author and illustrator, was born on August 30, 1938. He wrote and illustrated <u>Ten Black Dots</u> and <u>Freight Train</u>. He often includes himself in his book illustrations.

August 31

Maria Montessori was born on August 31, 1870. She was unhappy with the way young children were educated so she began her own school. She believed children could learn naturally through their environment.

Note: *Answers given to questions in italics are for information only.*

September Answer Key

September 1

World War II began on September 1, 1939, when Adolf Hitler and his German army invaded Poland. Almost 40 million people were killed in this war.

September 2

The great fire of London broke out on September 2, 1666. Within a few days, it had destroyed four-fifths of the city. What country is London? (Answer: *England, Great Britain, or the United Kingdom*)

September 3

The United States and Great Britain signed the Treaty of Paris on September 3, 1783. This treaty ended the American Revolution and made the United States a free country.

September 4

Spanish settlers founded Los Angeles in what is now California on September 4, 1781. It was originally named El Pueblo de Nuestra Senora la Reina de los Angeles, which means "The Town of Our Lady, the Queen of the Angels."

September 5

Jesse James was born on September 5, 1847, in Kearney, Missouri. He and a group of bandits spent their lives robbing trains, banks, and stores. They robbed their first train in 1873.

September 6

On September 6, 1941, all Jews over the age of six who were living in German territories had to wear yellow Stars of David on their clothes whenever they went outside.

Note: Answers given to questions in italics are for information only.

September Answer Key *(cont.)*

September 7

A very famous artist named Grandma Moses was born on September 7, 1860. She didn't begin painting until she was 78 years old, but she lived to be 101.

September 8

On September 8, 1921, the first Miss America was crowned. Her name was Margaret Gorman, and she was only 15 years old. Some people think there shouldn't be any more beauty pageants. What do you think?

September 9

California became the 31st state in the United States on September 9, 1850. Its capital is Sacramento, and it is known to have many earthquakes.

September 10

Elias Howe patented his lockstitch sewing machine on September 10, 1846. It sewed 250 stitches a minute. Unfortunately, he couldn't get anyone interested in buying it until much later.

September 11

On September 11, 2001, terrorists hijacked airplanes and flew them into the World Trade Center and the Pentagon. Many people were killed, including firefighters and police officers. Thank your local firefighters and police officers today.

September 12

The Lascaux cave paintings were discovered in France by four teenagers and a dog on September 12, 1940. The paintings are 17,000 years old and from the Paleolithic period.

September 13

On September 13, 1788, Congress authorized the first national election and selected New York City as the temporary capital of the United States. What is the capital of the United States today? (Answer: *Washington, D.C.*)

Note: Answers given to questions in italics are for information only.

September Answer Key *(cont.)*

September 14

On September 14, 1814, Francis Scott Key wrote the "Star-Spangled Banner" during the war of 1812. In 1931, President Herbert Hoover signed a bill making it the national anthem.

September 15

Tomie dePaola was born on September 15, 1934. He is a children's book author and illustrator who writes about his experiences as a child. He won the Caldecott Honor Award for his book entitled Strega Nona.

September 16

The Pilgrims left England on the Mayflower on September 16, 1620. When they arrived in America, they settled in Plymouth, Massachusetts. They were seeking religious freedom.

September 17

On September 17, 1787, the men attending the Constitutional Convention signed the Constitution of the United States. This document set up our government and our laws.

September 18

George Washington laid the cornerstone of the U.S. Capitol building in Washington, D.C., on September 18, 1793. Members of Congress meet in the Capitol to discuss and make our country's laws.

September 19

Jim Abbott was born on September 19, 1967, in Flint, Michigan. He was born without a right hand but became a major league baseball pitcher. He also won a gold medal in the 1988 Olympics, pitching for Team USA.

September 20

On September 20, 1519, Ferdinand Magellan set sail from Spain on a voyage around the world. He was killed during the voyage, but 18 men and one of his ships returned to Spain. This was the first circumnavigation of the globe.

Note: Answers given to questions in italics are for information only.

September Answer Key *(cont.)*

September 21

Hurricane Hugo hit Charleston, South Carolina, on September 21, 1989. A hurricane is a large rotating storm that forms over warm ocean waters. Hurricane season lasts from June through November.

September 22

President John Kennedy signed an act that established the U.S. Peace Corps on September 22, 1961. Men and women join the Peace Corps to help people in other countries and to learn more about other cultures.

September 23

On September 23, 1846, Johann Galle discovered the planet Neptune. It is the eighth planet from the sun and takes 165 years to revolve around the sun.

September 24

Jim Henson was born on September 24, 1936. He was the creator of <u>The Muppets</u> and <u>Sesame Street</u>. He designed Kermit the Frog, Bert and Ernie, and many other muppets for these television shows.

September 25

The explorer Vasco Nunez de Balboa crossed a small strip of land known as Panama on September 25, 1513. He sighted the Pacific Ocean and claimed the ocean for Spain.

September 26

John Chapman, who was also known as Johnny Appleseed, was born on September 26, 1774. He traveled across Pennsylvania, Ohio, Kentucky, Illinois, and Indiana planting apple trees.

September 27

Samuel Adams was born on September 27, 1722. He was an American patriot who helped to organize the Boston Tea Party. He also signed the Declaration of Independence and served as the governor of Massachusetts.

Note: Answers given to questions in italics are for information only.

September Answer Key *(cont.)*

September 28

According to legend, on September 28, 490 B.C., a Greek soldier ran 26 miles from Marathon to Athens in Greece to deliver a message that the Greeks had defeated the Persians. This is how the word "marathon" came to be.

September 29

The United States established the first regular army of 700 men on September 29, 1789. Since this time, many men and women have given their lives for their country.

September 30

On September 30, 1861, William Wrigley, Jr., was born. He was the founder of the Wrigley Chewing Gum Company and the owner of the Chicago Cubs baseball team. Wrigley Field in Chicago is named after him.

OCTOBER

October Answer Key

October 1

On October 1, 1971, Walt Disney World in Orlando, Florida, opened. Then, on October 1, 1982, Epcot Center opened at Walt Disney World. At the Epcot Center, you can learn about energy, dinosaurs, plants, and different countries of the world.

October 2

Happy Birthday, Charlie Brown! The first "Peanuts" comic strip appeared in newspapers on October 2, 1950. Charles Schultz created it. The last "Peanuts" comic strip appeared on February 13, 2000.

October 3

After World War II ended, the Berlin Wall was constructed to divide Germany into two countries, East and West Germany. The two countries were reunited on October 3, 1990, when the wall was taken down. At that time, the country resumed using the original name Germany.

Note: Answers given to questions in italics are for information only.

October Answer Key *(cont.)*

October 4

On October 4, 1957, the Soviet Union launched the first man-made satellite into orbit. It was called <u>Sputnik I</u> and traveled around the earth once every 96 minutes.

October 5

Chester Arthur was born on October 5, 1830. He was the twenty-first president of the United States. He became president after James Garfield was shot and killed.

October 6

On October 6, 1927, the first full-length talking movie was released. It was called <u>The Jazz Singer</u>, and it starred Al Jolson. By 1930, movie studios were no longer making silent movies.

October 7

Desmond Tutu was born on October 7, 1931. He won the Nobel Peace Prize and spoke out against apartheid in South Africa. Apartheid is a system that has different laws for blacks and whites.

October 8

The Great Chicago Fire started on October 8, 1871, and destroyed one-third of the city. According to legend, the fire started when a cow in Mrs. O'Leary's barn kicked over a lantern.

October 9

The Washington Monument opened to the public on October 9, 1888. It was designed by Robert Mills and had elevators that carried visitors to the top in 12 minutes.

October 10

On October 10, 1942, James Marshall, the author of children's books, was born. He wrote the George and Martha books and illustrated <u>Miss Nelson is Missing</u>. He created Viola Swamp after a real teacher he had.

Note: Answers given to questions in italics are for information only.

October Answer Key *(cont.)*

October 11

Eleanor Roosevelt was born on October 11, 1884. She was the wife of President Franklin Roosevelt and traveled to Europe during World War II as an ambassador of goodwill.

October 12

On October 12, 1492, Christopher Columbus saw an island in the Bahamas that he named San Salvador. Columbus was looking for a shortcut to Asia and believed he had found one, but the Bahamas is actually off the coast of North America.

October 13

Construction began on the White House on October 13, 1792. George Washington laid the cornerstone of the house, but he didn't actually get to live there. Who was the first president to live in the White House? (Answer: <u>John Adams</u>)

October 14

On October 14, 1912, while Theodore Roosevelt was campaigning for president, he was shot in the chest. The papers in his vest pocket saved him, and he insisted on finishing his speech before going to the hospital.

October 15

On October 15, 1990, Mikhail Gorbachev won the Nobel Peace Prize. He was the president of the Soviet Union and helped to make the Soviet Union a more modern and democratic country.

October 16

Noah Webster was born on October 16, 1758. It took him 50 years to plan, research, and publish his <u>American Dictionary of the English Language</u>. Many people still use Webster's dictionaries today.

October 17

On October 17, 1989, the Loma Prieta earthquake hit San Francisco, California. It occurred just minutes before the World Series was going to start there, and it caused $7 billion in damage.

Note: *Answers given to questions in italics are for information only.*

October Answer Key *(cont.)*

October 18

The United States flag was raised in Alaska on October 18, 1867. The U.S. had bought Alaska from Russia for $7.2 million. Many people thought that was too expensive, but they changed their minds when oil and gold were discovered there.

October 19

On October 19, 1860, an eleven-year-old girl named Grace Bedell wrote a letter to Abraham Lincoln, who was running for president. She told him he would look better with a beard, so he took her advice and grew one.

October 20

Herbert Hoover died at the age of 90 on October 20, 1964. He was the 31st president of the United States. He was president during the economic depression of the 1930s.

October 21

Alfred Nobel was born on October 21, 1833. He invented dynamite and had 355 patents for his many inventions. In his will, he left money to award Nobel Prizes to scientists, writers, and peacemakers.

October 22

General Sam Houston became the first president of the Republic of Texas on October 22, 1836. This was before Texas became a part of the United States. There is a city in Texas named for him.

October 23

The famous Brazilian soccer player named Pele was born on October 23, 1940. He played soccer for 22 years and scored 1,281 goals during his career. He encouraged many children all over the world to play soccer.

October 24

On October 24, 1901, a daring woman named Anna Edson Taylor rode inside a barrel over Niagara Falls. During this adventure, she fell 158 feet. When rescuers got to Anna, she said, "Nobody ought ever do that again."

Note: Answers given to questions in italics are for information only.

October Answer Key *(cont.)*

October 25

Richard Byrd, a famous Antarctic explorer, was born on October 25, 1888. He was the first man to spend the winter exploring Antarctica, the coldest place on Earth.

October 26

On October 26, 1825, the Erie Canal opened. It was cut through 363 miles of wilderness and was 40 feet wide. It allowed ships to travel from New York to the Midwest in order to trade goods.

October 27

The first subway, an underground railway system, began operating in New York City on October 27, 1904. Many people in New York still use the subway system as their main form of transportation.

October 28

The Statue of Liberty was a gift to our country from France. It was so large it had to be shipped to the U.S. in pieces. It was designed by Frederic Auguste Bartholdi and was first unveiled in New York Harbor on October 28, 1886.

October 29

On October 29, 1929, the stock market crashed, causing people to sell 16 million shares of stock. This was known as "Black Tuesday" and was the beginning of the Great Depression of the 1930s.

October 30

John Adams, our second president, was born on October 30, 1735. He was one of the authors of the Declaration of Independence, and he was the first president to live in the White House. His son, John Quincy Adams, became the sixth president.

October 31

The Mount Rushmore National Monument was completed on October 31, 1941. It is located in South Dakota. Which four presidents did Gutzon Borglum carve into the monument? (Answer: *Abraham Lincoln, Theodore Roosevelt, George Washington, Thomas Jefferson*)

Note: Answers given to questions in italics are for information only.

November Answer Key

November 1

On November 1, 1800, the White House became the official home of all U.S. presidents. John and Abigail Adams moved into the house even though it was not quite finished.

November 2

Daniel Boone was born on November 2, 1734. As an adult, he traveled from North Carolina to Kentucky, which was an unsettled area. He paved the way for thousands of pioneers to move to Kentucky.

November 3

On November 3, 1957, a dog named Laika became the world's first space traveler. The dog was on board a Soviet satellite called <u>Sputnik II</u>.

November 4

Iranian students who were followers of the Ayatollah Khomeini seized the U.S. Embassy in Tehran, Iran, on November 4, 1979. They held 52 Americans hostage for 444 days.

November 5

On November 5, 1872, Susan B. Anthony was arrested and fined $100.00 for trying to vote in a presidential election. She was released from prison but never paid the fine. She continued to work for the right to vote for women.

November 6

Adolphe Sax was born on November 6, 1814. He made musical instruments and was from Bulgaria. He invented a famous instrument. What instrument did he invent? (Answer: *He invented the saxophone.*)

Note: *Answers given to questions in italics are for information only.*

November Answer Key *(cont.)*

November 7

Franklin Delano Roosevelt became the first president to be reelected for a fourth term on November 7, 1944. Now presidents are only allowed to serve for two terms.

November 8

Montana became the 41st state to join the United States on November 8, 1889. The capital of Montana is Helena. Part of which national park is located in Montana? (Answer: *Yellowstone National Park*)

November 9

On November 9, 1938, Nazi soldiers destroyed Jewish synagogues, businesses, and homes in what became known as <u>Kristallnacht</u>, which means "Crystal Night." The soldiers sent 30,000 Jews to concentration camps.

November 10

The television show <u>Sesame Street</u> was shown on public television for the first time on November 10, 1969. It starred Big Bird, Oscar the Grouch, and Cookie Monster.

November 11

November 11 is Veterans Day. It is a day to honor all of those who have fought in wars for our country. It is celebrated on November 11 because the peace treaty ending World War I was signed on this day in 1918.

November 12

On November 12, 1954, Ellis Island in New York Harbor closed. This island had been used since 1892 to process 20 million immigrants as they entered the United States.

Note: Answers given to questions in italics are for information only.

November Answer Key *(cont.)*

November 13

The Vietnam Veterans Memorial was dedicated in Washington, D.C., on November 13, 1982. The memorial was designed by Maya Ying Lin and is a long, polished, black wall that lists the names of soldiers killed or missing in the Vietnam War.

November 14

On November 14, 1907, the children's book author William Steig was born. He didn't begin writing until he was 60 years old. His most famous book is <u>Sylvester and the Magic Pebble</u>.

November 15

The Continental Congress adopted the Articles of Confederation on November 15, 1777. This document united the 13 colonies and led to the writing of the U.S. Constitution.

November 16

Indian Territory and Oklahoma Territory were combined and Oklahoma became the 46th state on November 16, 1907. What is the capital of Oklahoma?
(Answer: <u>Oklahoma City</u>)

November 17

The Suez Canal opened in Egypt on November 17, 1869. It connected the Mediterranean Sea with the Red Sea. The canal made it much easier for ships to reach the Middle East and Asia, without having to sail around Africa.

November 18

Happy Birthday, Mickey Mouse! On November 18, 1928, Mickey Mouse was first seen in a black-and-white cartoon called <u>Steamboat Willie</u>. Walt Disney got the idea for Mickey from two real mice that scampered across his drawing board.

Note: *Answers given to questions in italics are for information only.*

November Answer Key *(cont.)*

November 19

James Garfield, our 20th president, was born on November 19, 1831, in Orange, Ohio. Before he became president, he worked as a janitor, teacher, preacher, and general. He was shot and killed while he was president.

November 20

African-American inventor Garrett Morgan received a patent for the traffic light on November 20, 1923. He invented it after seeing an accident between a carriage and a car. In what order are the lights on a traffic light? (Answer: <u>red on top</u>, <u>yellow in the middle</u>, and <u>green on the bottom</u>)

November 21

On November 21, 1620, the men on the <u>Mayflower</u> signed the Mayflower Compact. This was an agreement that they would rule themselves and not be ruled by a king.

November 22

Lee Harvey Oswald assassinated President John F. Kennedy on November 22, 1963, in Dallas, Texas. There has always been a lot of controversy surrounding Kennedy's death.

November 23

Franklin Pierce was born on November 23, 1804. He was the 14th president of the United States. The North and the South were becoming divided over the issue of slavery during his presidency.

November 24

A very famous jazz pianist and composer named Scott Joplin was born on November 24, 1868. He wrote "The Entertainer" and "Maple Leaf Rag." His music was not recorded until after his death.

Note: Answers given to questions in italics are for information only.

November Answer Key (cont.)

November 25

Children's book author and illustrator Marc Brown was born on November 25, 1946. He wrote books about Arthur the Anteater, his most famous character. In Marc's stories, Arthur even has his own television show.

November 26

On November 26, 1863, President Abraham Lincoln proclaimed that Thanksgiving should be celebrated every year on the last Thursday in November. Sarah Josepha Hale persuaded Lincoln to make Thanksgiving a national holiday.

November 27

Kevin Henkes was born on November 27, 1960. He writes and illustrates books for children. He has written Lilly's Purple Plastic Purse, Chrysanthemum, and Owen.

November 28

On November 28, 1895, J. Frank Duryea won the first U.S. auto race between gasoline-powered automobiles. Duryea's average speed was 7.5 miles per hour, and he won $2000.00.

November 29

Louisa May Alcott was born on November 29, 1832. She wrote a very famous book entitled Little Women. Many of the stories in the book are based on her life. This book was later made into a movie.

November 30

Samuel Clemens, who is better known as Mark Twain, was born in Florida, Missouri, on November 30, 1835. He was a reporter during the Civil War and later wrote famous books such as Tom Sawyer and Huckleberry Finn.

Note: Answers given to questions in italics are for information only.

December Answer Key

December 1

On December 1, 1955, an African-American woman named Rosa Parks was arrested because she wouldn't give up her seat on a city bus to a white person. African Americans in Montgomery, Alabama, decided to boycott the buses until they were treated fairly.

December 2

David Macaulay was born on December 2, 1946. He is a children's book author and illustrator who has always been interested in the way things work. Some of his books are <u>Cathedral</u>, <u>City</u>, and <u>Pyramid</u>.

December 3

Illinois became the 21st state on December 3, 1818. It has the sixth highest state population in the United States. Its largest city is Chicago, but the capital is Springfield.

December 4

Wassily Kandinsky was born on December 4, 1866. He was a Russian artist, and he is considered the first abstract painter. Abstract art is the opposite of realistic art.

December 5

Happy Birthday, Walt Disney! Disney was born on December 5, 1901, in Chicago, Illinois. He studied art and moved to Hollywood to make movies such as <u>Mary Poppins</u>, <u>Peter Pan</u>, and <u>Fantasia</u>.

December 6

On December 6, 1941, Franklin Delano Roosevelt made a personal appeal for peace to Emperor Hirohito of Japan. Roosevelt was trying to keep the United States out of World War II.

Note: Answers given to questions in italics are for information only.

December Answer Key *(cont.)*

December 7

Japanese bombers launched a surprise attack on Pearl Harbor in Hawaii on December 7, 1941. In the attack, the Japanese sank 18 ships, destroyed 200 planes, and killed 3,700 people. President Roosevelt said, "It is a day that will live in infamy."

December 8

The United States entered World War II on December 8, 1941. Congress declared war on Japan one day after the attack on Pearl Harbor. The U.S. later entered the war in Europe also.

December 9

Roller skates were patented on December 9, 1884. They were first invented in Holland, but they were patented in the United States. The first roller skates were very similar to today's rollerblades.

December 10

Melvil Dewey was born on December 10, 1851. He was an American librarian, and he invented the Dewey Decimal System. This is the number system used to classify non-fiction books.

December 11

On December 11, 1816, Indiana became the 19th state. There is a very famous car race held in Indiana's capital city. What is the name of this race?
(Answer: *Indianapolis 500*)

December 12

Guglielmo Marconi received the first transatlantic radio signal on December 12, 1901. He had been experimenting with radio waves since 1895, and he later opened the first wireless telegraph service.

Note: Answers given to questions in italics are for information only.

December Answer Key *(cont.)*

December 13

On December 13, 1642, the Dutch navigator and explorer Abel Janszoon Tasman discovered New Zealand. The country of Tasmania and the animal known as the Tasmanian devil are named after him.

December 14

On December 14, 1911, the Dutch explorer Roald Amundsen was the first man to reach the South Pole. He went on this expedition after he lost the race to the North Pole to Matthew Henson and Robert Peary.

December 15

U.S. soldiers killed Sitting Bull in South Dakota on December 15, 1890. Sitting Bull was a famous Sioux chief who did not want to live on a reservation, which is a place where Native Americans were forced to live after white settlers took their land.

December 16

The Boston Tea Party took place on December 16, 1773. American colonists were upset because the king of England was taxing them for tea and other items. They protested by dressing up as Indians and dumping a shipload full of tea into Boston Harbor.

December 17

On December 17, 1944, the United States ended the internment of Japanese Americans. After the attack on Pearl Harbor, the U.S. government removed many Japanese Americans from their homes on the West Coast and forced them to live in internment camps.

December 18

The U.S. Congress adopted the Thirteenth Amendment on December 18, 1865. This amendment officially ended slavery after the Civil War.

December 19

On December 19, 1843, Charles Dickens published his book entitled <u>A Christmas Carol</u>. In this story, a man named Scrooge learns the true meaning of Christmas after being visited by ghosts from the past, present, and future.

Note: Answers given to questions in italics are for information only.

December Answer Key *(cont.)*

December 20

South Carolina became the first state to secede from the United States on December 20, 1860. Ten other states later seceded. They formed their own country called the Confederate States of America and elected Jefferson Davis as their president. This led to the Civil War.

December 21

After a very long journey from England, the Pilgrims landed at Plymouth, Massachusetts, on December 21, 1620. They had been sailing on the <u>Mayflower</u> for over three months.

December 22

The Continental Congress established the Continental Navy on December 22, 1775. Esek Hopkins was made the commander of the Navy, which consisted of seven ships.

December 23

On December 23, 1823, the famous poem, "A Visit from St. Nicholas," was first published. Clement C. Moore wrote the poem. The first line is, " 'Twas the night before Christmas . . ."

December 24

The United States and Great Britain signed a peace treaty that ended the War of 1812 on December 24, 1814. In this treaty, the U.S. and Great Britain pledged to put an end to the Atlantic slave trade.

December 25

Christmas is the festival celebrating the birth of Jesus Christ and is observed on December 25 by Christians in most countries. Some traditions associated with this holiday are decorating an evergreen tree and hanging stockings.

Note: Answers given to questions in italics are for information only.

December Answer Key *(cont.)*

December 26

December 26 is the first day of Kwanzaa. African Americans celebrate Kwanzaa by lighting a candle each day until January 1. Each candle represents a Kwanzaa principle like unity and faith.

December 27

Another holiday that is celebrated at this time of year is Hanukkah, a Jewish holiday that lasts for eight days. Jewish people light a candle on the menorah for each of the eight days. The dates for this holiday change every year. In some years, it is on this date.

December 28

Iowa became the 29th state to be admitted to the Union on December 28, 1846. Iowa is bordered by both the Missouri River and the Mississippi River. What is the capital of Iowa? (Answer: *Des Moines*)

December 29

President Andrew Johnson was born on December 29, 1808, in a two-room shack in North Carolina. He took over as president after Abraham Lincoln was assassinated.

December 30

Children's book author and illustrator Mercer Mayer was born on December 30, 1943. He has written over 300 books, but he is most famous for his Little Critter books.

December 31

On December 31, 1907, the first ball was lowered at Times Square to celebrate the New Year. It has been a tradition ever since. The ball is made of Waterford crystal and weighs about 1,070 pounds.

Resources

Books

Hopkins, Lee Bennet, and Misha Arenstein. *Do You Know What Day Tomorrow Is?* Scholastic, Inc., 1990.

Learning Magazine's Day by Day All-Year-Long Book. Springhouse Corporation, 1993.

Thompson, Bobi. *Take Five Minutes: 365 Calendar-Related Editing Activities.* Teacher Created Resources, Inc., 1999.

Web Sites

Daily Almanacs

http://www.dailyalmanacs.com/almanac2.html

Encarta: On This Day

http://encarta.msn.com/features/onThisDay.asp

History Channel

http://www.historychannel.com/today/

Library of Congress: Today in History

http://lcweb2.loc.gov/ammem/today/today.html

PBS: History

http://www.pbs.org/neighborhoods/history/

Scope Systems: Any Day in History

http://www.scopesys.com/cgi/today2.cgi

The History of Today

http://www.on-this-day.com/

This Day in History

http://kids.infoplease.lycos.com/cgi-bin/dayinhistory

Timelines of History

http://members.theglobe.com/algis/